MUSICES OPUSCULUM

MUSICOLOGICAL STUDIES & DOCUMENTS

ARMEN CARAPETYAN
General Editor

NICOLAUS BURTIUS

MUSICES OPUSCULUM

PUBLICATIONS OF THE
AMERICAN INSTITUTE OF MUSICOLOGY

MUSICOLOGICAL STUDIES & DOCUMENTS

37

NICOLAUS BURTIUS

MUSICES OPUSCULUM

Introduction and Translation
by
CLEMENT A. MILLER

AMERICAN INSTITUTE OF MUSICOLOGY
HÄNSSLER-VERLAG
1983
67.737

Hänssler-Verlag, D 7303 Neuhausen-Stuttgart
Order-No. 68.737
ISBN 3–7751–0659–6

TABLE OF CONTENTS

INTRODUCTION

This edition of *Musices Opusculum* is based principally on the unicum printed for Burtius at Bologna in 1487. Of particular value is the copy preserved in the Biblioteca Palatina of Parma[1], which contains handwritten annotations and musical examples which are included in the present edition. The Bibliothèque Royale in Brussels (MS II 785, ff. 41v-44v) contains a manuscript entitled *Tractatus pulcher* which corresponds to Book II of *Musices Opusculum.* The Brussels MS is somewhat truncated and out of order. The MS, for example, begins with Ch. 2 of Book II, while only the second part of Ch. 1 is found on f. 43v. Folios 44r-44v contain a series of contrapuntal examples which Burtius apparently had considered using to illustrate the text of Book II on counterpoint. These examples, which are written in plainsong notation in the MS, are transcribed into modern notation in the present edition. Since Burtius says in Book I, Ch. 21, and Book II, Ch. 3, that musical examples are lacking in his work because the printers did not have the necessary musical characters, it is likely that the handwritten examples in Parma *Incun. 132* and in Brussels MS II 785 belong in a complete edition of Burtius' treatise.

A reprint of Burtius' Latin text, edited by Giuseppe Vecchi, was published in 1969 at Bologna.[2] Another Latin edition, which collates the material of the Parma imprint and the Brussels MS, was made in 1975 by Giuseppe Massera.[3] A Latin edition of the Brussels MS, edited by Massera, appears in *Quadrivium* VIII (1967), pp. 33-49, Bologna.

Although the Parma copy of *Musices Opusculum* and the Brussels MS contain handwritten musical examples which are illustrations of the printed text, it is clear that the original manuscript used by Burtius is now missing.[4] In his imprint of 1487 Burtius states, as already mentioned, that many musical examples are not included because the printers did not have the requisite musical characters, although he had prepared

1 *Incun. 132.*

2 *Musices Opusculum,* in *Biblioteca Musica Bononiensis,* II, 4. This edition is based on a copy in the Civico Museo Bibliografico Musicale in Bologna.

3 *Florum Libellus,* in *Historiae Musicae Cultores* 28, Florence. Although Burtius entitled his work *Musices Opusculum,* he calls it *florum libellus* in his description of the treatise.

4 See Massera, *Florum Libellus,* p. 48f.

numerous musical examples for his publication. The original printed edition not only lacks this material but also contains many errors and lacunae in the typography. None the less, the treatise contains one composition by Burtius which is the earliest known complete piece of printed polyphonic music.

Musices Opusculum should not be considered as an isolated treatise on music but as a part of a series of musical tracts and letters which convulsed the Italian musical world during the latter part of the fifteenth and the first half of the sixteenth centuries. A catalyst for the often bitter struggle between opposing musical concepts is the *Musica Practica* by Ramis de Pareia.[5] This astute and mordant Spaniard proposed many changes in current musical thought, including the removal of Guido's hexachord system through the introduction of an octaval system, a different method of tuning by applying the ratios 5:4 and 6:5 to major and minor thirds, and greater use of chromatic tones in contemporary music. His attack on John Hothby, the Carmelite monk and follower of Guido, produced three treatises[6] by the English theorist defending his position.

In 1487, the year of Hothby's death, Burtius took up the cudgels against Ramis with *Musices Opusculum.* This attack was countered in 1491 by Ramis' pupil and staunch supporter, Giovanni Spataro, in his *Honesta defensio in Nicolai Burtii parmensis opusculum.*[7] Spataro also sent a copy of Ramis' treatise to Franchinus Gaffurius in Milan, who returned it to Spataro with comments which were mostly critical, since he rejected the innovations proposed by Ramis. In 1520 Gaffurius wrote an *Apologia adversum Ioannem Spatarium,* and in the following year Spataro defended himself and Ramis in two publications, *Errori de Franchino Gafurio da Lodi* and *Dilucide et probatissime Demonstratione.*[8] In 1531 Spataro published a *Tractato di Musica*[9] (already complet-

5 Edited by J. Wolf in the *Internationale Musikgesellschaft, Beihefte II* (Leipzig, 1901). Since the spelling of Ramos for Ramis does not occur until the end of the sixteenth century, the present edition will refer to the Spanish theorist as Ramis.

6 "Three Treatises Against Bartholomeo Ramos", ed. A. Seay in *Corpus Scriptorum de Musica* 10, (Rome, American Institute of Musicology, 1964). They are *Excitatio quaedem musicae artis per refutationem, Dialogus in arte musica,* and *Epistola.*

7 Reprint in *Johannis Spatarii Opera Omnia,* I, ed. G. Vecchi, (Bologna, 1963).

8 Edited with German translation by J. Wolf from the Paul Hirsch Library (Berlin, 1925).

9 Reprint in *Biblioteca Musica Bononiensis,* II, 14, ed. G. Vecchi,(Bologna, 1970).

ed in 1523) which was a further attack on the musical principles of Gaffurius. Although Spataro and Gaffurius corresponded for many years, it is unfortunate that these letters are lost. But the most significant points of the entire controversy are mirrored in MS 5318 of the Vatican Library, which contains over 100 letters by Spataro, Aron, del Lago, and many others.[10]

From this short summary of the polemics and arguments that engaged Italian musicians during these many years, it is evident that Burtius' treatise belongs to the earlier stages of the dispute. Although Burtius called himself a professor of music and a student of pontifical law, he was also a priest,[11] writer, mathematician, and probably an astrologer, since the concluding chapter of *Musices Opusculum* is devoted to astrology. His principal activities as a practical musician occurred from 1503 until after 1518 while he was a guardacoro at the cathedral of Parma. Here he directed the choir and intoned the chants sung at canonical hours.[12]

In his musical treatise Burtius relied heavily on the *Ritus canendi* by Joannes Gallicus, his teacher.[13] He not only frequently quoted Gallicus verbatim but also adopted his phraseology. When Gallicus addressed himself "to the poor clerics and religious,"[14] Burtius did the same in his letter of dedication. The frequent mention of plainsong as "angelic chant" derives from Gallicus, just as the term "tolerable dissonances" for thirds and sixths. A number of the woodcuts in *Musices Opusculum* come from the treatise of Gallicus. While Gallicus referred to his readers as *carissimi,* Burtius called the same group *amantissimi.* Only in regard to the alleged inventor of consonant sounds did Burtius disagree with Gallicus. When Gallicus stated that these intervals were discovered by Jubal,[15] Burtius said that the Bible and the historian Josephus did not support this conclusion and the credit should go to Pythagoras.

10 For a study of these letters see K. Jeppesen, "Eine musiktheoretische Korrespondenz des früheren Cinquecento," *Acta Musicologica* XIII (1941), pp. 3-39.

11 For details of his life see Massera, *op. cit.,* p. 9ff.

12 Regarding the office of guardacoro, see *ibid.*, p. 33ff.

13 See E. Coussemaker, *Scriptorum de musica medii aevi* (Paris, 1876: reprint Hildesheim, 1963), IV 298-421. References to Gallicus' treatise are noted in the present edition.

14 *Ibid.,* 345.

15 See Coussemaker, *op. cit.,* IV, pp. 300, 310f.

Musices Opusculum opens with an aggressive and violent attack on the teachings of Ramis, whom Burtius generally calls a prevaricator, although this term is one of the more polite epithets he applies to the Spanish theorist. The vehemence of his assault on Ramis is truly a reflection of the seriousness and importance with which theorists in both camps viewed the musical controversy. Burtius' ire was aroused above all by Ramis' proposal to scrap the six Guidonian vocables and to replace them with eight other syllables[16] based on an octave. This constituted, in Burtius' opinion, an attack on ecclesiastical approbation of Guidonian doctrine and also on Guido himself,[17] whom Burtius considered to have been divinely inspired in the creation of his vocables.[18] If Ramis' system were adopted it would mean a complete revision of the traditional pedagogy of music and would also end the use of hexachords as a compositional device. Since Ramis' doctrine threatened to undermine a long established musical tradition Burtius opposed Ramis with all the strength he could muster.

But Burtius was concerned principally with the preservation of the six Guidonian vocables and not with the system of mutation which was not fully developed until several centuries after Guido.[19] Gallicus, although a follower of Guido, rejected the somewhat complicated principles of mutation and proposed a simpler use of the vocables.[20] This is probably the reason that his pupil, Burtius, took a rather ambivalent position on mutation. In I, 18, he says that some intelligent men have little use for mutation, but that he would treat the subject briefly. He states that either Guidonian vocables or letter names are applicable, and in I, 13, where he presents a diagram of the seven hexachords, he shows the notes alone without their corresponding vocables, thus avoiding a direct presentation of mutation, although in the text he indicates that the vocables are to be used.

16 *Psallitur per voces istas.* See Wolf, *op. cit.*, p. 19.

17 Ramis said that Guido was probably a better monk than a musician. *Ibid.*, p. 11,

18 For further material on these points see Edward E. Lowinsky, *Music of the Renaissance as viewed by Renaissance Musicians* (Ohio State University Press, 1966), p. 158f.

19 See for example Hieronymus de Moravia, *Tractatus de Musica,* in Coussemaker, *op. cit.*, I, 22.

20 Coussemaker, *op. cit.*, IV, 377.

In the *Honesta defensio* of 1491 Spataro launched a vigorous counterattack against Burtius. An examination of some parts of this work is helpful in illuminating certain aspects of *Musices opusculum,* although sometimes the statements of the two men are in such complete opposition that it is difficult to uncover the actual facts. Although Spataro tells Burtius to accept the work as instructive for him and not as an invective,[21] the Bolognese musician attempted to demolish Burtius in much the same way that Burtius tried to discredit Ramis.

Spataro claimed that Burtius was ignorant of the principles of music, and that when Burtius showed Ramis some of his compositions which allegedly were contrapuntally incorrect, Ramis humbly advised Burtius not to make public his songs until he had studied a little.[22] As further proof Spataro cited Don Zohanne Antonio Peccora, a singer at San Petronio, to whom Burtius had shown some of his compositions. Burtius in turn, in the dedicatory letter of *Musices Opusculum,* stated that in Bologna he had given a book by Guido to Ramis, who however, did not understand it.

Since these charges and countercharges were the result of personal encounters involving Burtius, Ramis, and Spataro, it would be very helpful to know when they occurred, but this point is still not settled. Although Spataro was born in Bologna and Burtius probably went there in 1472,[23] the date of Ramis' arrival in that city is not known. According to Palisca,[24] Ramis came to Bologna no later than 1472, a statement which may be true but which is unsubstantiated.[25] It is also possible that Ramis spent all or part of 1472–1482 in Florence.[26] At any rate, by 1482 when Ramis was in Bologna, and his treatise had been

21 *Honesta defensio,* f. A 2(r).

22 *Ibid.,* f. A 3(r). Regardless of the veracity of this statement it seems questionable that Ramis would "humbly" advise anyone!

23 Massera, *op. cit.,* p. 9.

24 "Ramos de Pareja", *Die Musik in Geschichte und Gegenwart,* vol. 10, col. 1909.

25 The source is supposedly J.Wolf, editor of Ramis' treatise, but Wolf was careful not to be explicit on this point. Wolf's words are: . . . spätestens 1472 Ramis Salamanca verlassen hat. 1482 treffen wir ihn in Bologna. See Ramis' *Musica Practica,* ed. J. Wolf, XIII.

26 See A. Seay, "The *Dialogus Johannis Ottobi Anglici in arte musica",* in *Journal of the American Musicological Society,* VIII (1955), p. 91; *ibid.,* "Florence: The City of Hothby and Ramos", IX (1956), p. 193 ff.

published, Burtius' claim that he did not understand Guido was no longer valid, as is evident in the *Music Practica,*[27] although Burtius may have been referring only to Guido's contributions and not those of his followers. On the other hand, Spataro's statement concerning Burtius' ignorance of music was also no longer valid in 1487, when the latter's treatise appeared, for it contains both the conventional rules of counterpoint and a three-voice composition by Burtius which is contrapuntally accurate in every detail.

In defending Ramis' ideas Spataro attempted to denigrate the Guidonian contributions. He pointed out that Guido's antiphonary was approved by Guido's order but not by the Church as a whole.[28] Yet Guido had gone to Rome and shown the antiphonary to the Pope, who evinced great interest in it and wished Guido to remain in Rome and instruct the clergy there. Only Guido's inability to withstand the Roman climate caused him to leave.[29] The pope in question here is not Pope Benedict, as Spataro believed,[30] but Pope John XIX (1024–1033).[31]

Since Burtius based most of his statements about Guido on the treatise of his teacher Gallicus, some of Spataro's refutations are more properly directed against him. This is especially true when Spataro[32] accused Burtius of taking a passage at the beginning of Ch. 14 from Ramis' treatise. The reference is to the tetrachords as the basis of a melody. A comparison of the treatises of Burtius and Gallicus shows that Burtius borrowed this passage almost literally from Gallicus[33] rather than from Ramis. In a similar case Spataro criticized Burtius' definition of *proprietas* in Ch. 19, saying that "according to this reasoning there will be not merely three *proprietates* but seven."[34] But Burtius'

27 See Wolf, *op. cit.*, pp. 11f, 19. Ramis included the Guidonian hand and mutation, both of which originated after Guido's death.

28 *Honesta defensio,* B 7(v).

29 *De ignotu Cantu Epistola,* in Gerbert, *op. cit.*, II, 44a.

30 *Op. cit.*, B 8(r).

31 See Gerbert, *loc. cit.*, also "Guido von Arezzo", *Die Musik in Geschichte und Gegenwart,* 5, col. 1072.

32 *Op. cit.*, C 1(r).

33 See Coussemaker, *op. cit.*, IV, 375a.

34 Secundo quaesta rasone non seranno solamente tre proprieta ma septe *Op. cit.*, D 1(v).

definition of *proprietates* comes primarily from Marchettus.[35] although he also makes use of material from Tinctoris.[36]

Spataro offered a refutation or "correction" for every reference Burtius made to Ramis. Some of these proposed improvements are more significant than others, and some show the convolutions indulged in by many theorists in making their points. An example of the latter is Spataro's answer to Burtius' statement in I, 23: "the above tropes can have a fourth or four vocables below and an octave above, in which case they are perfect... If they exceed this range a little they are not superfluous as the prevaricator (Ramis) says, but are called pluperfect according to the authority of Joannes the Carthusian and others."

The dispute here would seem to center on the point that Ramis called an excessive melodic range superfluous *(superfluus)*,[37] while Gallicus said it was pluperfect *(plusquam perfectus)*.[38] But Spataro ignored this aspect and stated[39] that according to Boethius modes and tropes were octave species. He then gave the Guidonian rule for the authentic and plagal ranges, saying that Burtius contradicted Guido. Spataro's intent was to show that a trope was one of the eight modes and that Burtius had not defined their ranges according to the precepts of Guido.

This apparent conflict is resolved by noting that Gallicus and Burtius considered a trope to be one of the four *maneriae*,[40] which included the range of an authentic mode and its plagal, or an octave and a fourth, as Burtius stated. The idea that modes were tropes came from Guido who said: *Hi sunt quattuor modi vel tropi.*[41] Spataro's statement[42] that Burtius did not give the Guidonian range for an authentic mode is also refuted in I, 23, where Burtius states Guido's rule for these modes.[43]

35 See his *Lucidarium* in Gerbert, *op. cit.*, III, 91a.

36 See his *Tractatus de musica*, Coussemaker, *op. cit.*, IV, 7b.

37 Wolf, *op. cit.*, p. 55.

38 Coussemaker, *op. cit.*, IV, 353a.

39 *Op. cit.*, D 4(r).

40 This is evident from the title and text of I, 23.

41 See *Guidoni Aretini Micrologus*, ed. J. van Waesberghe, *Corpus Scriptorum de Musica* 4 (American Institute of Musicology, 1955), p. 133.

42 Ecco come lo tuo Guido dice che lo auctento non descenda se non uno voce sotto il finale: perche aduncha tu ignorante dici diathessaron. *Op. cit.*, D 4(v).

43 Hi (the authentic modes) etenim usque ad diapasson ascendere tenentur: possunt tamen iuxta regulas guidonis unam sub suo fine deponere vocem.

In the introduction to Book II Burtius defined counterpoint as simple song in a certain way doubled or tripled. Spataro questioned this definition, asking if simple and duple in relationship to counterpoint are not mutually opposed.[44] Again the source of the definition is Gallicus,[45] and it refers to simple song or plainsong sung with other voices, but exclusively in note against note style. The latter is important, for Burtius' five contrapuntal rules (based on Gallicus) and their examples are all note against note. When Burtius said in II, 3, that only perfect consonances can begin a composition, Spataro commented[46] that Burtius' own mensural composition in II, 5, did not follow that rule but began with a major third.

This may reveal an inconsistency in Burtius, although it may also indicate that he felt a mensural song could be less strict, since he made a clear distinction between note against note counterpoint and rhythmically free mensural music.

It is worth noting in Book II on counterpoint that Burtius called 3rds, 6ths, 10ths, and 13ths by two names: (a) imperfect consonances and (b) tolerable or compatible dissonances. It would seem that the first phraseology was preferable to Burtius for he entitled II, 1, "perfect and imperfect consonances", and his illustration of these intervals used the same nomenclature. But in defining the five precepts of counterpoint he used the terms "compatible dissonances" for imperfect consonances. Since he derived his precepts from Gallicus,[47] he used Gallicus' terminology for these intervals, which was *dissonantiae compassibles,* in deference to his teacher.

According to Spataro the fifth precept of Burtius came literally from Ramis.[48] Since the opening proposition of the fifth precept is a direct quote from Gallicus,[49] Spataro's statement is not wholly accurate. But he is correct concerning the second part of the precept relating to the organization of counterpoint in the manner of a *fuga.* This material is clearly drawn from Ramis.[50]

44 Simplice e duplicato non sonno contrarii? *Op. cit.*, D 7(v).

45 Coussemaker, IV, 38b.

46 *Op. cit.*, D 8(r).

47 Coussemaker, *op. cit.*, IV, 384b.

48 Da quello che tu dici e nota sino a lultima littera di questo tuo quinto precepto tu lhai ad litteram tolto dal mio Pareia fonte delli musici. *Op. cit.*, D 6(v).

49 Coussemaker, *op. cit.*, IV, 395a.

50 See Wolf, *op. cit.*, pp. 67, 68.

Although Spataro had many "corrections" to make concerning Burtius' Book III on mensural music, one of the most significant occurs in III 13, on *proportia tripla,* since it relates to a fundamental difference between Spataro and many other theorists including Gaffurius. In III, 13, Burtius says that singers incorrectly consider sesquialter proportion as *tripla.* Spataro's "correction" states:[51] "this number can be either the one or the other, that is, *tripla* or sesquialter ... for in these signs 03, C3, ⊙. Ͼ, it will always be tripla, but in 02, C2, 0, C, it will always be sesquialter." The entire matter is relative to Spataro's belief concerning a breve's value, which he based on Ramis.[52] According to Spataro a breve was *the* basic note and had the same unchangeable temporal value in both *tempus perfectum* and *tempus imperfectum.* Thus a perfect breve in O would consume the same amount of time as an imperfect breve in C. In modern terms, if a breve is considered the equivalent of a measure, then a measure in triple meter would have the same temporal value as a measure in duple meter. As a corollary of this a semibreve in O would move at a different rate of speed than a semibreve in C.

As already mentioned, Spataro wrote an entire treatise on the subject of sesquialter.[53] In it he harked back to the *antiqui* for corroboration and presented his own thesis of the immutability of the breve and the application of sesquialter to musical practice. His work primarily opposes the theories of Gaffurius, although Tinctoris also comes in for criticism.[54]

In III, 20, 21, Burtius described the tuning of organs and other keyboard instruments. He limited the range of his keyboard to the fifteen strings of the Greek disdiapason, although he stated that many more pitches could be added by doubling at the octave. Using Pythagorean

51 questa cifra medesima po fare luno e laltro zoe tripla: e sexquialtera . . . perche in questi signi. O 3. C3. ⊙ . Ͼ. sempre fara tripla: ma questi. O 2. C2.O . C. sempre fara sexqualtera. *Op. cit.,* Fl.

52 Wolf, *op. cit.,* p. 77.

53 *Tractato di musica . . . nel quale si tracta de la perfectione da la sesquialtera . . .* Venice, 1531.

54 As in Ch.16: Ma dove Franchino dice: che Tinctoris non fa alcuna differentia in tra la minima di questi segni punctati ⊙ . Ͼ . e la minima di questi segni non punctati. scilicet O / C : el se concede che Tinctoris habbia havuto tal opinione: ma esso Tinctoris resta pero incolpato da la mera verita.

intonation only, he first tuned the fifteen white notes. Then the black keys were added, but only as flats. They were numbered as follows:[55] 1st B♭ ; 2nd *d*♭ ; 3rd *e*♭ ; 4th *g*♭ ; 5th *a*♭. A 6th black key, a higher *b*♭, was included to show the principle of octave doubling.

In commenting on this tuning Spataro rightly questioned the lack of sharps, and gave an example which would require a *c*♯.[56] What Burtius did was to use exactly the tuning procedure given by Gallicus,[57] although the latter recognized the possibility that sharps could also be used.[58] There is also an interesting relationship between Gallicus, Burtius, and Gaffurius regarding this tuning. In the *Theoricum musicae* of 1480, Gaffurius followed the tuning method of Gallicus exactly. Burtius did the same, but his wording of the tuning follows Gaffurius very closely. Thus part of the text of III, 21, of *Musices Opusculum* is a literal repetition of the second part of *Theoricum musicae* V, 5, although both theorists used Gallicus as their source.

Burtius applied the principle of successive counterpoint to musical composition. The order of voices to be composed depended on the function of the music. In a secular song the soprano would be written first, then the tenor, and finally the lowest voice. In a piece based on a plainsong the tenor would be first, the soprano next, and the lowest voice last. This technique of course, was rooted in much earlier practice. An early fifteenth century manuscript,[59] probably referring to fourteenth century music, states that in a motet the tenor should be composed first, but in rondeaux, virelais, and ballades the soprano should be written first. The practice of vertical or simultaneous composition developed during the course of Burtius' life. Apparently it first received theoretical approbation in the *Musica* of 1507 by Johannes Cochlaeus, who said that all voices could be composed at the same time,[60] although

[55] In arriving at these pitches Burtius used his compass in this order: 1st *B* ♭ ; 3rd *e*♭ ; 5th *a*♭ ; 2nd *d*♭ ; 4th *g*♭ .

[56] *Op. cit.,* F7 (v).

[57] Coussemaker, *op. cit.,* IV, 317-323.

[58] *Ibid.,* IV 322f.

[59] Cambridge, Corpus Christi College MS 410, II, f. 7v. See M. Bukofzer, "Fauxbourdon Revisited", *The Musical Quarterly,* XXXVIII (1952), p. 38.

[60] Fol. E IVr. *Possunt autem omnes partes simul componi.* Cochlaeus also stated that experienced composers could write individual parts separately, but that it was important for students to compose the voices together on a ten-line staff, since they were not yet completely knowledgeable about concords and cadences. Ten-line staves are used in the *Musica* to illustrate contrapuntal concords and cadences.

generally the tenor was written first. In 1516 Aron[61] called simultaneous composition the new method of composing.

A valuable contribution to improvised singing is found in II, 6, of *Musices Opusculum.* It is particularly helpful because it is clear and straightforward, which is not the case with some other writers on this subject.[62] According to Burtius this procedure, which he learned as a child, was used daily in royal chapels, especially in France. The object was to organize note against note counterpoint against plainsong written on a four-line staff. The rules were made up by the singers and were unrelated to the precepts of composition.

In the first rule, when the tenor or plainsong descends, the organal voice ascends through a unison, third, fifth, sixth, and octave. But this is only the visual aspect of the organal voice since it is sung an octave higher. In this way the two voices actually begin on an octave and move in contrary motion through consonant intervals to a double octave.

The second rule demonstrates the consonant intervals available in double counterpoint at the octave, and is used when the plainsong ascends. In this case the organal voice is visually below the plainsong and makes a unison, third, fourth, sixth, and octave with it. In singing it sounds above the plainsong, and makes an octave, sixth, fifth, third, and unison with it. Burtius concludes by saying that the rules, which can be used in various ways, were presented for those readers who wished to sing organal music against plainsong.

In viewing Burtius' treatise as a whole, it seems clear that he was not an innovative music theorist, but rather a defender of the traditional and the orthodox. This is especially true concerning the Guidonian vocables and the majority of the principles espoused by Gallicus,[63] the teacher of Burtius and the main source of the latter's treatise. Burtius was primarily a compiler of a compendium on music in which, he stressed, he would present the essentials of music and strive to avoid

61 In *De Institutione Harmonica.*

62 See for example Simon Tunstede (Coussemaker, IV, 200) and Guillelmus Monachus (*Ibid.*, III, 273).

63 Some writers consider Burtius to be a pupil of Ramis, but Burtius never acknowledged this. Although both he and Spataro in all likelihood attended lectures of Ramis, Burtius' views and those of Ramis were so divergent that the former probably was not his pupil and certainly not his disciple.

anything superfluous. It is, as he said, an enchiridion in which many aspects of music culled from many sources are treated in summary form.

Burtius displayed a considerable knowledge of medieval and classical literature which he coupled with references to pontifical and Roman law, an area in which he considered himself proficient. His frequent allusions to Persius, Cicero, Pliny, Aristotle, and other classical authors confirm his knowledge of ancient classical literature. Christian writers include Lactantius, Isidore of Seville, Albert Magnus, and of course, Boethius and Guido d'Arezzo. Like so many Renaissance writers Burtius was loath to admit his dependence on his contemporaries. Two exceptions are Gallicus and Ramis, although the latter is mentioned only in a critical way. Yet, as mentioned earlier, Burtius knew the *Theoricum musicae* of 1480 by Gaffurius and probably several treatises by Tinctoris. The entire tone of *Musices Opusculum,* despite the diatribes against Ramis, reflects the thoughts of a writer who is humanistically oriented. Even the patriotic, almost chauvinistic praises he sings of Italy in I, 28, express one aspect of the emerging humanism of the age.[64] It is probable that Burtius' humanism results from association with Gallicus, who had studied grammar and the music of Boethius under the humanist Vittorino da Feltre (c. 1378–1446).

Apparently Burtius enjoyed substantial acclaim as a theorist among his contemporaries. The entire first part of I, 28, on tropes or modes, is quoted in a treatise[65] by Bonaventura of Brescia, who founded a music school in that city in the latter part of the fifteenth century. He also shows the division of a whole tone according to Burtius. Stephanus Vanneus[66] quoted Burtius as an authority on the finals of the modes. In the dedicatory letter to Bartolomeo Maschara of Brescia, Lanfranco[67] calls Burtius "mio Burtio Parmegiano." He is also named in an anonymous Venetian music treatise.[68]

64 See A. Buck, "Humanismus", *Die Musik in Geschichte und Gegenwart,* 6, col. 883.

65 *Brevis collectio artis musice,* MS A 57 in the Civico Museo Bibliografico Musicale, Bologna.

66 In *Recanetum de musica aurea,* Rome, 1533, I. p. 31.

67 In *Scintille di Musica,* Brescia, 1533.

68 See Massera, *op. cit.,* p. 37.

Burtius displays the same eclectic procedure in Bk. III on mensural music that characterizes much of his treatise. The first two chapters of Bk. III, for example, clearly show the influence of Ramis,[69] while the chapters immediately following on ligatures, rests, alteration, and diminution follow the *Libellus cantus mensurabilis* of Johannes de Muris.[70] In Ch. 9 on syncopation Burtius gives two definitions of the term, the first from the *Libellus* and the second apparently derived from Prosdocimus de Beldemandis.[71] Ch. 11 on numbers is indebted to Isidore of Seville, and the chapters on proportions and the various genera depend on Boethius, but most particularly on Gallicus, who may be considered the principal source of Burtius' *Musices Opusculum.*

Clement A. Miller

[69] See Wolf, *op. cit.*, p. 78f.

[70] See Coussemaker, *op. cit.*, III, 52a, 55b, 57a, 58a.

[71] See Coussemaker, *op. cit.*, III, 224a.

CHAPTER HEADINGS

Book I

Chapter

Book II

Book III

MUSICES OPUSCULUM

A little musical work by Nicolaus Burtius of Parma, professor of music and very studious of pontifical law, begins with a defense of Guido d'Arezzo against a certain prevaricator.

Nicolaus Burtius sends best greetings to poor clerics and religious.

Many years have passed into the shadows of adolescent days since I expended much time on the discipline of music in nightly toil, and many have received a beginning and development in this study through me. Now, dearest friends, having been overcome by your loving kindness and by the exhortations of certain friends, I have set forth my vigils for you who in greater measure have the talent to proclaim this doctrine. For what is more reasonable than to dedicate ingenious works to those who are superior to all others in ability, learning, and worthy esteem? I am aware that I am undertaking a rather difficult subject and that I am exposed to the disparagement of many men, although this disparagement means little to the truly learned. But since in former times this depreciation irritated the men of highest authority, what can I expect, whom neither authority nor merit will protect? Yet I am joined to the one who sings through the psalm writer: Open your mouth and I will fill it.

And so, before I express our own views, I decided to overcome the errors and ignorance of a certain modern writer and to demonstrate to everyone clearly and fully that they are erroneous concepts. For with scoffing and entirely false ineptitudes he tries to oppose the pious Guido d'Arezzo, who is deservedly preferred through sanctity and philosophical learning. O extraordinary calumny! O impudence unheard of before today! Again and again he raves and cries out with many invectives. What are you shouting, what is tormenting you? Before I leave this it is necessary that you feel ashamed of your most nefarious error. For this man wrote a little book on the study of music[1] in which, when he wanted to explain what Boethius meant in his five books, he was very clearly confused and thus subverted every arrangement

1 *Musica Practica Bartholomei Rami de Pareia,* ed. J. Wolf (Leipzig, 1901).

of value and principle. Moreover, he not only attacks Guido but also scolds, abuses, and torments with a certain doglike barking all those he knows to be followers of Guido. At times he praises the Carthusian monk Joannes,[2] who extols Guido with the strongest praises in his work. What a contradiction!

At one time while in Bologna you read by yourself a book by Guido which you received from me and which you did not understand. The ignorance of the man, the conceit of the man! For at the beginning of his work, where he examines the division of a monochord (which is complete confusion), he says that he had read thoroughly the teachings of the ancients in many vigils and with considerable labor, since he wished in this way to avoid the errors of modern writers.

Do you not see, I ask, how worthless, how arrogant, how impudent, is the criticism of this man? Where is Boethius, the monarch of musicians, who shows such a division with the most excellent ratios? Where is the very common division of Guido and Joannes, the Carthusian? For no one is so young or so simpleminded to whom such a designation is unknown. I also will not omit the crass teaching of this man about the principles of music in which, as a result of nocturnal study, he said that he would apply new syllables to individual strings.

The syllables are described by him in this way: *Psal-li-tur per voces is-tas.* The connection of such a pattern is *Psallitur per voces istas.* What madness, what unbearable ignorance! Examine it yourself. For you describe in a varied and almost useless way singing among the ancients, while we have read this in a complete form in a codex of Boethius in the library of St. Dominic in Bologna. If what you have found in Odo and the Enchiridion, as you write, you esteem little, you cite the latter incorrectly, since the book is a manual and apochryphal. Why don't you want others than you to perceive this? For among the former these were the names of notes: *Noe noa anne cane agis,*[3] just as we have the syllables of Guido. But others wrote them thus: *Tri po de nos tri te,* which have the same meaning as the first. The

[2] Joannes Gallicus, author of *Ritus canendi vetustissimus et novus.*

[3] See Aurelianus, *Musica Disciplina,* in Gerbert, *Scriptores* (St. Blaise, 1784), I, 42; also E. Werner, *The Psalmodic Formula Neannoe and its origin,* in *The Musical Quarterly* XXVIII 1942, p. 93. For *Tri, po, de . . .* see J. Wolf, *Handbuch der Notationskunde* (Leipzig, 1913), I.56.

Carthusian Joannes has discussed all of them thoroughly, for they were invented before the time of St. Gregory. If afterwards Gregory wished to use only seven Latin letters, as often as they need to be repeated, and since Ambrose and Augustine preferred to follow these footsteps rather than follow strange ones[4], why do you not blush to pervert and deprave this order in your censorial arrogance? Are you perhaps holier or finer or more skilled than these pillars of the church? Why do you not rather follow these church fathers if you do not wish to embrace the teaching of Guido? You are insolent, you are arrogant and a prevaricator, as everyone can easily see. Your ignorance need not be shown as much as your perverseness must be demonstrated. For the teaching of a pious monk, which has spread throughout the world with ecclesiastical approval and by means of the wonderful invention of notes, is going to persevere, in spite of your maliciousness. Its sweetness, its easiness, and its enjoyment seem naturally inborn in the minds of men. What then am I to conclude about you, since I could adduce and disprove many things which for the sake of time and place are removed from our treatise? If you understand me with a sound mind you will take care that all examples which are the result of your perversity are either burned or, if someone can bear so much labor, are emended, so that the studies of so many religious are not defrauded in the future in their value through your error.

And thus, dearest friends, please forgive me if the insolence of this father of an ox has led me away from you, so that when I wrote to you I digressed from a single point to create almost an entire oration. If in it I was sometimes provoked to irritation, I bear witness to the virtue that I did not do this willingly but through necessity.

Description of the book.

Our compendium, which is based on three tracts, is called *florum libellus* because it contains what should be learned in a worthy writing and a foundation to any such work. Also, where anything superfluous

[4] In A 64, a copy of *Musicies Opusculum* at the Civico Museo Bibliografico Musicale of Bologna, the following contemporary (Latin) gloss is found: This is an error because Ambrose and Augustine lived long before Gregory.

and erroneous has been said by that irrational man it will be refuted with every effort and truly clear reasons.

In our first tract I will show first what music is and praises concerning it. Second: the various kinds of music; what a musician is and the difference between a musician and a singer. Third: what sound is and a general definition of sound; what a tone is, how it is formed, and what is consonant or dissonant. Fourth: I will explain what harmony is, who produced music in the beginning, and the three genera of melody; then I will show what the order is of learning music and how it should be begun. Fifth and last: what the connections or intervals of music are and which are more necessary; what tropes or modes are, by whom they were invented, and what our understanding comprises.

In the second tract we will treat what makes mixed song, which is commonly called counterpoint, and we will explain, after rejecting the opinions of certain singers, how it is easily composed. The third treatise, which comprises the end of our book, concisely includes figured song, the value and rhythm of notes, also numbers, proportions, and the division of a monochord.

Dearest friends, these things created for you with immense labor from codices of distinguished writers and through our own industry, will be an introduction for each of you to the higher goals you wish to reach. Wherever all aspects could not be treated it seemed worthwhile to me at least to bring together in a brief summary the explanations made by some in many volumes, so that more protracted and excessive explanations do not vanish from a listener's mind, remembering the Horatian precept: Whatever you teach, be brief, so that docile minds may quickly grasp and faithfully hold the words; everything in excess escapes the saturated mind.[5]

I ask, therefore, that you read our work willingly. If you have read it thoroughly from beginning[6] to end and also have memorized it, I truly expect that within three months you can be numbered not among the singers, which is less important, but among the musicians, which is most important. If certain things seem rather intricate to you, you

[5] Horace, *Ars Poetica,* 335.

[6] Corrected from *calce* in Parma *Incun. 132.*

should remember that "no art can be understood by books alone without an interpreter and without some practice."[7] Farewell, and pray for me to the one and only Trinity.

Chapter 1

What music is and whence it is named.

Just as Cicero said at the end of the book called *De universo:*[8] It is necessary for anyone who considers himself a lover of intelligence and wisdom to seek the primary causes of the nature of understanding and wisdom, and then to investigate[9] their secondary causes. I believe this is what we must do, namely, to discover what music is, as afterwards I will come to its application.

"Music is an art pleasing to God and man. It distinguishes and determines everything that is sung, and it searches for the true reason for all things which occur through arsis and thesis, that is, through the rise and fall of tones."[10] It is named from the Greek muses, meaning inquiry. As Isidore said, the reason is because at that time the modulation of tone and the use of songs were being sought, or as pleasing to some, because antiquity invented music through the nine muses. So also poets created the muses as daughters of Jupiter and Memoria because sounds die away unless committed to memory, since they could not be written down. By some writers music was named from Moys [Moses], which is water, because as they say, music at first was sought in water and moist areas, which is entirely false and erroneous, for it is openly condemned by Joannes the Carthusian at the close of his work and in many other places. It is never found, dearest friends, in early philosophers or in Boethius, but as I believe, in certain irrational writers. May they then grow dumb, for they are truly confused.

7 Cicero, *Epistulae ad Familiares* 7, 19.

8 *Timaeus,* 14.

9 Burtius' version differs here from the original.

10 From Joannes Gallicus, *Ritus canendi vetustissimus et novus,* I, 2, in Coussemaker, *op. cit.*, IV, 300.

When music is found in its proper context it will agree with the clearest ratios, for the elements of this discipline are consonances, proportions, and parts of proportions, as a whole tone, semitone, ditone, and similar intervals which move to a consonance, as will be shown very fully later. Just as arithmetic is the ratio of numbers, and geometry of sizes, and astrology of the movements, sizes and distances of heavenly bodies, so music is the movement of sounds.

Chapter 2

Praises of music.

In former times the art of music was highly esteemed among the Greeks, so that no one was considered fully educated unless he were able to sing and play string instruments. Thus from Valerius Maximus in *De studio et industria*[11] we read that Socrates learned to play string instruments at an advanced age, believing it better to study the art late in life than never to know it. Just as he learned while an old man he bade talented youths be instructed in the art, not as an incitement to pleasure but to govern their emotions by rule and reason. For not every tone which sounds well causes such an emotion, not all who are equipped with reason attain a truly harmonious life. The study of music has great value to refresh the spirit and to quiet the passions; a knowledge of this discipline is worthy of an honorable talent.

For this reason we will examine the various natures and powers of sounds, and the consonances and dissonances which result from them. Thus Aristotle in *Problems* taught well that music is naturally pleasurable and that it is a friend to every kind of moral character. Did not David, as it is found in Book I of *Kings,*[12] free Saul from an evil spirit by the art of music? Did not the physician Asclepiades often restore to sanity the delirious minds of those disturbed by sickness, as in Celsus' *De medicina* III, 18, on three kinds of insanity?

[11] VIII, 6,8.
[12] I *Kings,* 17, 23.

Nowhere do we read about such a severe and hard heart that it was not moved by effect of emotions of this kind. So one reads in Valerius Maximus in Book 2 on ancient customs that in sumptuous banquets elderly Romans sang extended poems to high-pitched pipes, so that by imitation they restore their more active youth. This is corroborated by Cicero's opinion in the beginning of the fourth question of *Tusculanae.* [13] A lyre or cithara was passed around at a banquet and convivial songs were sung by those reclining at table. We also intermingle such songs in our times. Nicomachus, a teacher of arithmetic, deservedly treated music. Also the geometricians Archytas and Aristoxenus have shown it the highest reverence. As Cicero says in Book 6 of *De republica,* the theologian Plato found the sweetest harmony of the world in the sense of hearing. Finally, from a Grecian proverb it is still proclaimed that the unlearned dislike music.

What more shall I say? It is not remarkable that music is so pleasurable among men, since such birds as goldfinches, nightingales, and others make great use of song as though having a knowledge of the art. Does it not cause dolphins to take pleasure in hearing song? Solinus states this in *Collectanea,* [14] and Pliny in Book 9 where he describes their lives. The fable was deservedly invented that Orpheus and Amphion influenced irrational animals, stones, and trees with their music. Some musical instruments move the mind to pleasure, but others move it to rage, as we will speak later about musical instruments.

Thus musical harmony eases the fatigue of all labors, soothes the mind, delights the spirit, but also excites the emotions and produces rage. It calms the woodlands, it placates the weary, and its practice allows those occupied with labor to tolerate it easily. Enough has been said about the praises of music, although I could spend much more time extolling it. Now I come to the threefold division of music.

[13] IV, 2.
[14] Ch. 21.

Chapter 3

The kinds of music.

Just as Boethius in *Musica* I, 2, said that music was threefold,[15] so we, following in his footsteps, say that the first is called cosmic, the second human, and the third instrumental because it was created for certain instruments. The first kind is called cosmic because it includes the entire universe, so to speak. For the universe is formed with a certain harmony and the heavens are moved in a harmonious modulation. But the intervals of celestial bodies are considered only by reason and not by sense. Thus, according to Macrobius, Pythagoras thought the distance from earth to moon was about 126,000 stades, and that this was the interval of the whole tone. The length of a stade is made clearer in the third tract, where we discuss the roots of successive quantities.

An interval is the distance between a high and low sound. From the moon to Mercury is a large semitone because it consists of two dieses and one comma, as will be seen more clearly later. From there to Venus, which is given various names, as by Pliny in Book 2 of *Historia Naturalis,*[16] is almost as large, namely a small semitone, because it consists of only two dieses. A diesis is half a comma. From there to the sun is a little more than three times the distance, namely a whole tone and a small semitone. So the sun is three whole tones and one small semitone from the earth, a distance which is called a fifth. For when we speak of connections a fifth consists properly of three whole tones and one small semitone.

From the moon to the sun is a fourth which consists of two whole tones and one small semitone. From the sun to Mars is the same interval as from earth to the moon, that is, a whole tone. From Mars to Jupiter is almost half of this, that is, a small semitone. From Jupiter to Saturn is a little larger interval, that is, a large semitone. From there to the top of the heavens, where the signs of the zodiac are, is a small semitone.

[15] See Boethius, *De institutione musica,* ed. G. Friedlein (Leipzig, 1867), p.187.
[16] In II, 6, Pliny names Lucifer, Vesper, Juno, and Isis.

And so from the heavenly ceiling to the sun located in the middle, the father of planets and men as it were, is a fourth. From the earth to this heavenly tip is five whole tones and two small semitones. These are inferred to be an octave, which is called a universal harmony, as in Book 2 of Pliny's *Historia Naturalis*,[17] where he writes on the music of the spheres. Yet ignorance must not be attributed to so great and excellent a man who described the fabric of the universe and anything in it that is comprehensible, because he wished an octave to be formed from seven tones, but rather it must be considered the error of a corrupted text, since an octave arising from only five whole tones and two small semitones is lacking in a comma for the small semitones, which do not make a complete whole tone.

But it could be said that he was following the opinion of Aristoxenus, as Macrobius very wrongly concludes in Book 2 of *Somnium Scipionis*. Through the same error the master reconciler[18] was deceived in the thirteenth *Problem* of Aristotle by concluding that the double octave is formed from twelve whole tones, from which an octave would contain six whole tones. For a disdiapason is a double octave.

Well spoken is Dorylaus' saying that the universe is the instrument of God. But why is its harmonious melody not heard, although the universe is always in motion? In answer some have said that such a sound or concord is so weakened in our ears from the moment of birth that it can scarcely be heard, just as it is clear that the din of those hammering is scarcely audible to them through habit. Others said it seems to be inaudible because of the size of its tone which the smallness of our ears cannot hear at all.

This has been shown in Cicero's *Somnium Scipionis* where he says:[19] Man's ears, which are full of this sound, have become deaf to it. There is no duller sense in you than hearing, for in the same way where the Nile rushes down to the place called Cataculpa[20] the people living there have lost their sense of hearing because of the volume of sound. But this sound, moved by the very rapid revolution of the universe,

[17] II, 20.
[18] Peter of Abano.
[19] *De Re Publica*, VI, 18, 19.
[20] Actually Catadupa, the Nile cataract.

is so powerful that human ears cannot perceive it, just as you cannot look at the sun, for our keenness of vision and sense of sight are overcome by its rays.

Again, earthly music is said to arise from four elements, which are treated in that fountain of eloquence called *De Universo,* for there everything is established clearly and very fully. So it happens that Cicero says that God put it among fire, water and air, and he compared these elements and connected them by proportion. Just as fire is to air so air is to water, and as air is to water so water is to earth. From this conjunction the sky is so moved that it falls under the sense of sight and touch. For this reason and from these elements numbering four the body is an earthly product formed, as he said, in that proportion.

From this he explains that the body is concordant in a certain friendship and love. And so will it remain in harmony, so that it cannot be loosened in any way except by that to which it is bound. O Cicero, who would doubt you, extolled by everyone as a man of distinguished thought, of prudence, and of sincerity? You have esteemed all morality and virtuous study; you would rejoice with someone such as Jerome if your death had not come so cruelly before the baptism of Christ.

Thus the four elements hardly combine at all their differences and opposing forces except that a certain harmony unites them into one body and one fabric. Yet all this diversity produces such a variety of seasons and produce that they form a cycle of only one year. For what winter binds spring relaxes, and what summer burns autumn ripens. Likewise here are the words of the poet in *Remedia amoris:*[21] Autumn gives apples, summer is beautiful in harvest time, spring offers flowers, winter is lightened by fire. So in turn the seasons either produce their own fruit or give aid to the others.

[21] Ovid, 187.

Chapter 4

Human music

Man is an animated body which is formed from four elements, which are earth, water, air, and fire, as in Lactantius, Book 2 of *Divinae Institutiones,* and in the first question of Cicero's *Tusculanae,* and also in his *De Universo,* likewise in the chapter *in quadam* on the most distinguished canonists. [22] Indeed, legists have a gloss in the preface of the *Institutionum* [23] at the words *prima elementa.* To strengthen such a connection the four elements are made similar to the four humors (blood, choler, phlegm, and melancholy).

Thus the Pythagoreans and Platonists taught that such an arrangement or connection was formed in a musical ratio. For just as a consonance in sound is a mixture of high and low tones reaching the ears sweetly and uniformly, as will be shown later, so the required connection of parts or the conformity of any organization is called a consonance. Pythagoras and Philolaus called man himself a harmony. In the first question of Cicero's *Tusculanae,* Socrates put this human music in the voice alone, but Aristoxenus placed it in the voice and in bodily movements. According to Lactantius in Ch. 16 of *De opificio Dei,* Theophrastus wrote that human music is active in the voice and in the movement of mind and body. Just as the mind is joined to the body by numbers, as in Book I of Macrobius on *Somnium Scipionis,* so also we do not hesitate to connect not only the mind to the body but also the elements and movements in musical harmonies (which are considered to be formed from numbers) in a natural arrangement and in a certain harmonious connection. So there is a statement of Herophilus, a most distinguished professor of the art of medicine, that when we say something we are actually affected by our own beating pulses, and that this act is shown to be associated through musical rhythms with the powers of harmony. So human music is the concordant connection of diverse elements in a single unit, namely in the human body.

[22] See *Decretals* of *Canon Law* X, 3, 41, 8.

[23] Justinian's *Institutionum,* in *Corpus Iuris Civilis* (Berlin, 1954), I, preface.

Chapter 5

Instrumental music.

Instrumental music is governed by different kinds of instruments, that is, those that are natural and those that are artificial. First I will explain natural instruments and then artificial instruments. Natural instruments, according to Albert Magnus in *De anima,*[24] Book 2, of the voice are the lungs, throat, palate, tongue, lips, and teeth, and these administer the duties of the human voice. So harmonic music, which includes and governs sounds produced by the human voice in a naturally combined instrument, is a notable art and a perfect science of song consisting of these parts, or sounds, words and numbers. Poets agree that the last named is meter. By considering the limits of time in a given ratio they investigate the measurement of various feet, as the dactyl, iamb, tribrach, and others.

It remains now to consider artificial instruments. Some of them are an incitement to pleasure, yet others induce animosity, anger, fury, and similar emotions. Those causing pleasure are the organ, monochord, psaltery, cithara, lyre, and an ensemble of pipers which the Romans used in the temple of Jupiter, as in the chapter on an ensemble of pipers in *De institutionibus antiquis* by Valerius, for they placated the anger of the gods and gave them the highest veneration. Our religion also does not cease to conciliate one God in the Trinity with songs and organs in constant laudations and prayers.

The triumph of pipers is attributed to Mars, the cithara to Apollo, pipes and other instruments of this kind are attributed to the muses. Instruments which cause animosity, anger, and fury are straight and curved trumpets, drums, and other instruments which create noise and din. The clangor of the instruments grew more powerful as the soldiers engaged more vigorously in battle. Thus the Spartan army was incited by musical modes.

I think it is unquestionably true that the renown of Rome in wars was superior to others. In our own time also it is known that in Liguria

[24] See *Alberti Magni Opera Omnia,* vol.VII, *pars* I (Aschendorff, Monasterii Westfalorum, Germany, 1968), Book 2, Tract 3, Ch.22.

under the leadership of Roberto Sanservino the enemy, numbering many troops, was terrified by the clangor of drums and trumpets, and was thrown into flight, and the entire army was captured as booty. Of the instruments played by blowing, those are subject to organized music which are played rhythmically by the application of fingers or the use of keys.

Chapter 6

What a musician is and the difference between a musician and a singer.

It was stated above what music is and what its praises and threefold division are. Now I will show very concisely what a musician is and the difference between a musician and a singer. Dearest friends, since the study of music is a natural science, and speculation or theory results in a superior and wiser understanding than practice, therefore a speculative musician is one who applies knowledge in considering singing not with the servitude of work but with the power of speculation. But if he spends time on practice he will not add a varied multitude of things to speculation, but rather its completion, and it should be known that through this he becomes a well-rounded musician who lacks nothing in speculation and in practice.

Speculation results from two causes, hearing and reason. Not hearing alone but reason also takes part in a definite judgment. Hearing is the beginning and in a certain way it holds a position of correction. But the final perfection of knowledge consists in reason, which adheres to certain rules and never falls into error. For we perceive consonances by ear, but the intervals by which they are separated we do not measure with our ears which are inexact in judgement, but with rules and reason. Thus according Boethius[25] a musician is someone who has the faculty of speculation and understanding of musical ratios, not someone who is concerned only with a practical way of singing. Yet a practitioner of this discipline is a singer who sings and does not know he sings. Also excluded from such speculation are string players, organists, and others who show

25 *Op. cit.*, I, 34; p. 224 in Friedlein edition.

their skill on instruments, since they are entirely lacking in theoretical reasoning. Poets also are drawn to song by a certain natural instinct rather than by speculation and reason, for our Boethius excludes them from musical speculation.

"So[26] a musician is to a singer as a judge is to a court crier, for the crier proclaims the judge's decisions without knowing why they were made, although the judge knows everything. Every musician is a singer but not every singer is a musician." Otherwise not only small birds, wild beasts, and small animals, but also the ignorant and unskilled singing by nature alone and without instruction would be musicians. Thus the speculative excels the practical, for it is much better and more worthy to know what one does than to carry out what another knows. Guido said there is a great distance between musicians and singers. The latter sing, the former know what music contains. For one who does what he does not understand is considered an animal.

Chapter 7

Sound and its general definition.

According to Albert Magnus in Book 2[27] of *De anima* sound is heard by the ears through the movement of air. But Boethius said sound is the uninterrupted movement of air striking the ears. According to rule in a general way everything that sounds or is heard can be called sound, but this is not strictly true. Some sound is noise, some ringing, and some echo. Noise is confused sound, as the sound of seas and floods. Ringing is properly the reflected sound of metals, as in cymbals and bells. Echo is sound which occurs in vaulted places or in enclosed valleys. Pliny speaks of this in Book 6 and Book 30 of *Historia Naturalis.* In Persius:[28] the Bacchic cry resounds and reverberant Echo responds. Now the differences of sound have been treated.

Pulse and percussion make sound, and this cannot occur without motion, that is, unless motion first precedes sound, as Albert says. So

26 From Gallicus, in Coussemaker, *op. cit.,* IV, 344.
27 *Op. cit.,* Ch. 18.
28 A. Persius Flaccus, *Satirae,* I, 102.

sound does not exist without motion, which is the cause of it. Motion is called a successive change occurring in time, as in Book 5 of *Physics.* Time is successive duration or the counting of motion. Some movements are faster, some more sluggish, and some slower. If one considers continuous motion it must be either fast or slow. Every slow and more widely spaced movement creates low sounds. But a fast and compact motion produces high sounds by propelling them with speed and velocity. Thus if we further tighten a taut string it will produce a high sound; when it is loosened it makes a low sound. Therefore a low sound arises from slower and more separated movements, and a high sound from quicker and closer movements. A lower tone is always imputed to weight and a higher tone to acuteness, as Marcus Tullius says in Book 6 of *De Republica.*

Some objects sound well, some poorly, and others add nothing. All, even solids,having sufficient air sound strongly. Compared with other objects metals are sonorous, especially gold, silver, and copper. When they are mixed together with a little water and earth, they are better than other metals; their earth is sulphur that has been extracted. Iron also contains much base material, so that it has a dull sound, yet because it is finer than lead and lead alloy, it rings more sharply than they ring. Lead and lead alloy have an almost stifled and dead sound because they contain more water. The makers of bells and organs temper and lower the highness of a sound made from copper by adding a portion of lead.

Flexible material does not sound well in that it does not react strongly, for it yields to a blow and quickly expels the air. There are materials which do not sound, as a sponge, which seems to drink in the air, retaining it rather than expelling it. The same is true of hair and wool, because they are thin and scanty, and therefore without sound. These are the principal points when we speak about sound.

Chapter 8

Vocal tone and its production.

According to Albert on the voice,[29] a tone is the movement of air exhaled in the *arteria* [30] *vocativa,* the vocal canal which is the organ of respiration. It is composed of hard rings and is connected to lungs, continually supplying air as if to bellows. According to Guido in Ch. 1 of his *Musicae,*[31] a tone is the audible percussion of air in the required amount. Or as some say, a tone is a beating of air. Since this is the same thing, these words have been used. If one asks by what it is struck, undoubtedly it is by the tongue. In Lactantius, *De opificio Dei,* Ch. 8, a voice is named from *auden,* that is from hearing *(auditus).* By the interchange of a letter *aures* are named as if *audes*; or *vox* is from a calling *(vocando),* for it expresses prayer with vocal chords.

The duties of the human voice are many and are expressed in diverse ways, as has been noted earlier on instrumental music. They are expressed by the tongue, the influence of four teeth, the repercussion of two lips, the hollow of the throat, and the assistance of the lungs. The latter, as Albert said, takes in and exhales air as if bellows. Some tones are continuous and others are suspended by an interval. A continuous tone is one we use to read prose narrative. A suspended tone is one men use to raise and lower sounds.

Chapter 9

Consonance, its formation, and dissonance.

Consonance is a mixture of high and low sounds striking the ears pleasantly and uniformly. Boethius [32] has stated this very clearly in this way: When two strings are stretched with one lower, and are struck together, they produce a certain mixed and sweet sound; the two tones

[29] *Op. cit.,* Ch. 22.
[30] *arteria* in Albert Magnus; *arataria* in Burtius.
[31] See M. Gerbert, *Scriptores* (St. Blasien, 1784: reprint 1963), II, 37.
[32] *Op. cit.,* I 28; p. 220 in Friedlein edition.

join together as one, and this is called a consonance. A consonance is a fifth, an octave with a fifth, and a double octave, as will be seen later when we consider mixed song. Consonance is named from "following", as Isidore says, because it organizes its tones successively. Euphony is the same as consonance, and is named from *eu* or good and *phonia* or sonority, making good sonority. We consider it the same as symphony.

Dissonance is the striking together of two mixed sounds coming to the ears with sharpness and unpleasantness, just as Boethius states: When two strings are plucked together and each wants to go its own way, without striking the ears pleasantly or uniting the two sounds into one, this is called a dissonance. Some dissonances are tolerable and others are intolerable. Tolerable dissonances are thirds, sixths, tenths, and similar intervals, to use the language of an ordinary singer. Intolerable intervals are those otherwise named *exmelles* or unpleasant, as fourths, sevenths, elevenths, and similar intervals.

Chapter 10

Harmony

As Lactantius says in *De opificio Dei,* Ch. 16, musicians call harmony the consonant stretching of strings[33] into a complete concord without causing dissonance. Cicero also, in the first questions of *Tusculanae Disputationes,* speaking on the soul against various philosophical opinions and especially against Aristoxenus, said musical harmony arises in intervals whose varied composition also forms many harmonies or consonances. Thus harmony is the appropriate union of different tones. Or it is a vocal modulation and a concord of many sounds, as is very evident in figured song, especially when we sing in three or four concordant parts. The same is true in artifical instruments. For when two of their strings are plucked so that one moves higher and the other lower, this is not really harmony but consonance or tolerable dissonance. Yet when many strings are plucked, this is what is called harmony. So Boethius said harmony is considered the concordant mixture of different tones, but music is the ratio of this concordance.

33 Here Burtius has *vocum,* while Lactantius has *nervorum.*

Chapter 11

The first man to sing and connect sounds in a musical proportion.

We see here from ancient books that many men were distinguished in music, as Orpheus, Amphion, Zethus, Mercury, Linus, Lyco, Architas, Aristoxenus, Ptolemy, and Timotheus. They were brillant in all kinds of music, for whenever it was appropriate they excited the minds of men to violent action by harmony, and again reconciled them to calmness and placidity.

But in preference to them I will present two others worthy of highest praise, yet without violating our regard for the aforementioned ancients. One is in the testimony of sacred Scriptures, namely Jubal. The other is Pythagoras, approved in Greek and Roman writings. As told in the beginning of Genesis,[34] Jubal was the seventh descendant of Adam in the lineage of Cain, and Moses said he was the father of those who plays organs. But he did not claim that Jubal was the inventor of consonances or proportions. Without wishing to be detrimental to Joannes the Carthusian, he wrote in his *Musica,* I, 1, 10, that according to Josephus, when Jubal learned through a prophecy that the world was endangered by fire or water, he immediately built two columns, one of bricks protected from fire, the other of marble protected from floods, and on them he carved the roots of all proportions and consonances which he heard on the hammers of his brother, Jubalcain. This, I believe, was invented by Johannes the Carthusian in order to honor the sacred Scriptures rather than human writings, since you do not find it anywhere in Josephus except concerning the sons of Seth, who described on the aforementioned columns the material and study of celestial bodies, which pertains to astrology.

After long cogitation Pythagoras discovered by investigation and reason that musical consonances were produced only through proportions, and later he showed them in rules and ratios. Previously they were perceived only by a corruptible aural sense, as ancient codices intimate, and as Boethius and Guido in the last chapter of his *Musica*

34 This entire passage is based on Gallicus, in Coussemaker, *op. cit.,* IV, 299, 310. The biblical reference is to Genesis 4, 21. Burtius took literally Gallicus' phrase *in organis*, although the modern translation is usually "pipe".

confirm. How do I explain such a development? It happened that Pythagoras was passing the shop of some smiths and the sound of hammers came to his ears. As it was his custom to investigate a perceptible relationship between the visible and the invisible, he ordered a change to be made because of the dissonance of one hammer, for there were five hammers and he wished to know whether the import to the sound resulted from the variety of hands. When this was done a pleasant concord immediately resulted. After removing one hammer he weighed the others by comparing them mutually. He discovered some produced a 2:1 proportion, some epitrite or 4:3, some 3:2, and some 9:8. For example, if one compares 12 pounds to 9, a 4:3 proportion results, 9:8 makes a sesquioctave, 12 to 8 makes 3:2, 8 to 6 makes 4:3, and 12 to 6 makes 2:1, as here:[35]

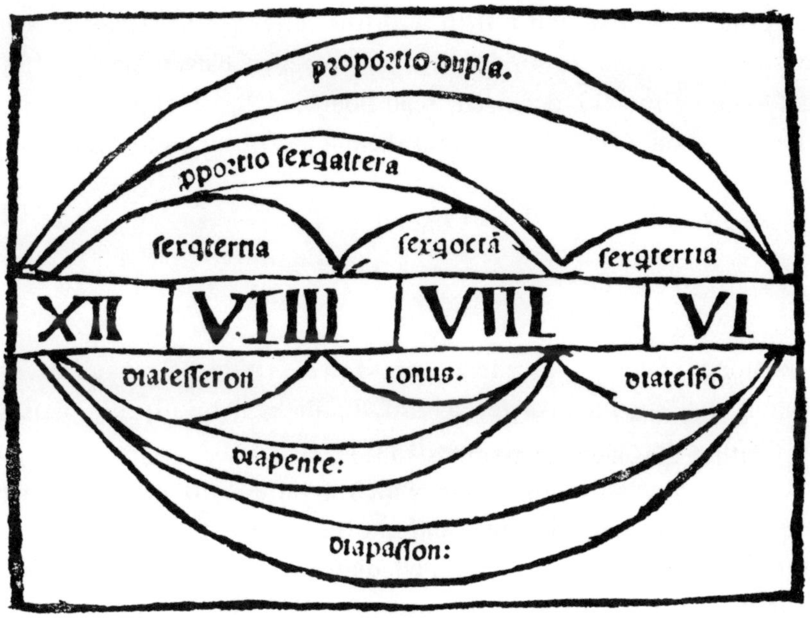

I will show how a fourth makes 4:3, a whole tone 9:8, a fifth 3:2, and an octave 2:1, in the third tract when we discuss proportions more fully. Pythagoras adapted proportional weights to the uniform strings truly approved for proportions. He also studied various instruments and

35 The diagram is based on Gallicus, in Coussemaker, *op. cit.*, IV, 311, although Gallicus attributes the discovery of these proportions to Jubal.

copper bells made in varying weights, striking them with a copper or iron rod and obtaining musical consonances from their proportions. As he wisely said, everything consists of measurement, numbers, and weight.

From this the reader can easily see that Jubal did not invent proportions and consonances, as some assert, but only played the organ and cithara, so that even in our times many have been misled in this regard. For at that time men were living in another manner on a newly-created earth and under new skies. You can see that the crass and awkward talents of men were useless for such inventions. Even after some time had elapsed music was still so very simple that it only consisted of four strings, whose inventor was Mercury according to Boethius. Thus a tetrachord was named from four strings.The first and fourth strings sounded an octave consonance. The middle strings made a whole tone together, and formed a fourth and a fifth with the outer strings. Later on Greek philosophers added to the strings and reached eleven strings. If you want to know how this occurred read Boethius, Bk. 1 of his *Musica,* and you will not only find this but also the names of the philosophers.

Chapter 12

Three genera of melody

Among philosophers there were three genera of melodies whose meaning was shown in a tetrachord. I will treat briefly the praises of the diatonic tetrachord, because it is the first truly perfect order. The first genus is called diatonic, in which a tetrachord moves through a small semitone, a whole tone, and another whole tone, with two such intervals. For I think it was called diatonic as if *dytonus* or moving naturally through these two intervals. Not only philosophers but mother Church selected the diatonic from the three genera because it is more fitting and natural than the others. In all songs it is the natural way that a fourth should be sung on four separate tones. It arises from two distinct whole tones and one small semitone, which is appropriate in this diatonic genus.

In the chromatic and enharmonic genera it is less fitting. For in the chromatic genus a tetrachord moves through a small semitone, a large semitone, and three semitones, of which one is larger or an apotome and two are conjuct smaller semitones, forming a semiditone. So each tetrachord in this genus reaches a consonant fourth, but not with the same inner structure as in the diatonic. It is called chromatic because it is changed from another *color,* for the Greek *chroma* is called *color* in Latin, so that the chromatic genus produces a tetrachord of another design.

In the enharmonic genus each tetrachord moved through diesis, diesis, and ditone. A diesis is half of a small semitone, as we will discuss later concerning parts of tones. An enharmonic tetrachord has this name because it is more closely connected than a chromatic tetrachord. Here is a description of all the tetrachords.

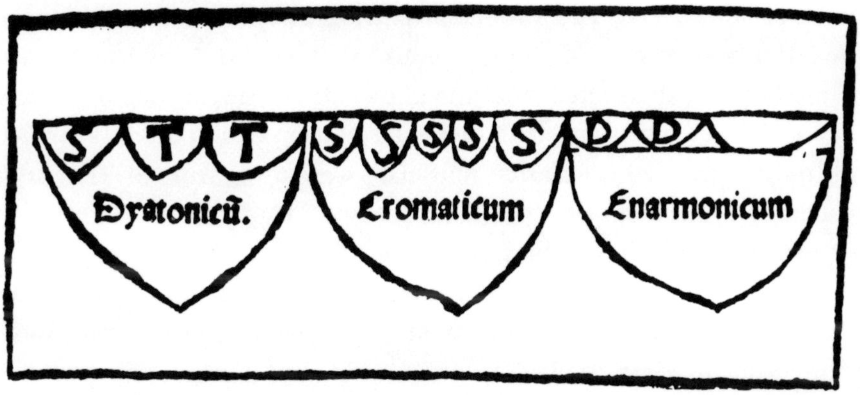

In the above genera each tetrachord forms a complete fourth, but with differing intervallic structures, as has been said. The chromatic and enharmonic genera have been discarded by musicians because of the difficulty in singing them. But the diatonic genus has been retained and preserved with the greatest veneration by Platonists, Pythagoreans, and other musicians because of its very pleasant and naturally arranged harmony. Now it is applied to an easy angelic song of plainchant, so that it is used by all singers and musicians with the exception of the prevaricator, who has applied not a new but rather an old form of singing, as is apparent in his writings.

Chapter 13

In what order should practical music be learned?

Since we have explained above the more important points about the three genera of melody, we will now treat in very concise language the order of the diatonic genus that is used by mother Church and the whole world, so to speak. First, dearest friends, let us learn thoroughly what must be studied in musical discipline based on the diatonic genus, not what belongs to antiquity or is learned from ignorant and unskilled singers, but only what is approved by the church. The pious Benedictine monk, Guido d'Arezzo, devised this under divine inspiration from his bishop, since in complete obedience he uncovered the complexities and in a wonderful way produced a method of such easiness. For earlier times used various ciphers, and ecclesiastical musicians used indications of notes; there were also various inventions in relation to teaching. In the letter he wrote to Michael,[36] monk of Pomposa,[37] and in Book 1 of his *Musicae,* it is stated that the knowledge of singing could scarcely be acquired in ten years. With divine inspiration Guido directly applied not only letters, which church musicians were using from St. Gregory's teaching, in the form of a left hand easily understandable to boys, but he also invented six vocables, *ut, re, mi, fa, sol, la,* from the hymn of St. John. Then using lines and spaces he developed a complete antiphonary which is presently used in the Roman Church. Pope John, reigning in his time, wished to examine it, and disregarding whatever other singers had invented, praised, retained, and confirmed it.[38]

Now, dearest friends, the folly and insolence of this Spaniard moves and provokes me to indignation. He has tried to cast a shadow on the very clear teaching of this most distinguished man among all talented men. Let him be silent and mute for he is deserving of hellebore. Returning to the subject, the manner in which Guido invented these things and used them in teaching is told to the monk of Pomposa in the same

36 See Gerbert, *op. cit.,* II, 43.

37 A Benedictine monastery at Ferrara where Guido was educated.

38 Most of the preceding material on Guido comes from Gallicus, in Coussemaker, *op. cit.,* IV, 373.

letter. This symphony is an example which I use from beginning to end in teaching boys.

As you see, six vocables result by extracting the first six syllables of each phrase, so that tyros and novices, as if supported by a staff, are able more easily to ascend and descend by whole tones and semitones, as in this example:

The Guidonian vocables taken from the hymn of St. John could be repeated endlessly if the human voice were not limited. Note that in ascending and descending, a whole tone always occurs between vocables except between *mi* and *fa,* which form a small semitone. Also in following the diatonic genus with the Gregorian letters, a small semitone always precedes or follows two whole tones. The positions of small semitones in Gregorian letters are *b c* and *e f.* These are called fixed or permanent according to the natural order of letters preceding or following two whole tones. A small semitone also occurs between *a* and round *b* when a tritone must be removed. This semitone is called moveable because it is changed according to need. Likewise semitones are called moveable which usually divide a whole tone when needed, namely, to perfect such composite intervals as an imperfect fifth or octave. We will speak about this later on mixed song. But in plainsong a moveable semitone occurs only in tempering a tritone, and musicians cannot avoid the harshness of a tritone in any other way. They have placed this key between mese and paramese.

Chapter 14

Why Guido selected only six syllables.

Surely[39] one should not wonder why Guido wished to choose only six vocables for singing and not the fifteen of many philosophers, or as many as were commonly used in their time, or only four, or more or less. Since Guido was a true musician he knew that everything sung was contained in four tones or two tones and one small semitone; the first fourth was called a complete tetrachord by ancient philosophers, that is, a composition of four strings. What do you sing beyond the first fourth that is not one and the same thing? Since there are four tones from the Greek gamma to low *c*, or two whole tones and one small semitone, which form one of the three kinds of fourths, you will have the same thing if you go a little farther from *c* to *f*, also from low *f* to round *b*, and so forth ad infinitum.

Thus this hexachord of Guido not only includes one fourth-species but also two other variations of the first arrangement, although the third fourth-species begins in the same way that the first one ends. If one begins the three fourth-species in *a* he will not be able to sing them in a sequence of six letters without incurring a very great confusion of tones. An example:[40]

[39] This chapter is based on Gallicus, in Coussemaker, *op. cit.*, IV, 375.
[40] The example follows Coussemaker, *op. cit.*, IV, 376.

You see very clearly how easy, accurate and pleasant such instruction is which includes all six notes of the Guidonian scale. It is useless to do by more what can be done by less.[41] For this series of six tones not only includes the three fourth-species as already mentioned, but also the first fifth- and fourth-species from which an octave harmony is formed. It also contains the five Latin vowels, without which nothing can be expressed correctly and suitably. In the first syllable of *ut queant laxis* etc., there is *u*, in the second *e*, in the third *i*, in the fourth *a*, in the fifth *o*, and in the sixth *a*, which is a repetition of the fourth. Thus there are five vowels, *a, e, i, o, u*. This is perfection in teaching.

I may not omit here the perfection of number six in relation to such a hexachord. For this is the first perfect number within ten, since six contains all its aliquot parts exactly. Aliquot parts are those which as often as they are taken produce their complete total. Twenty-eight is perfect within one hundred, and within one thousand, four hundred ninety-six is perfect.[42]

Number six is commended by canonists in the preface of the sixth book[43] at the word *senarius*, and in a gloss by Joannes Andrea, also by Augustine in *De Civitate Dei*, Bk. 11, at *haec quidem*. This has been said because of the arrogance of an irrational man who ventured to burst forth in a compendium of his confusion that the teaching of Gregory,

41 A favorite quotation by Renaissance writers, taken from Aristotle.

42 The aliquot parts or factors of 6 are 1, 2, 3, making 6; 28 has 1, 2, 4, 7, 14, which total 28; and 496 contains 1, 2, 4, 8, 16, 31, 62, 124, 248, which total 496.

43 *Liber Decretalium D. Bonifacii Papae VIII*, preface. Following the five books of decretals of Pope Gregory IX, Pope Boniface named his decretals the *Liber sextus* and called six a perfect number. Joannes Andrea (1275–1348) wrote a commentary on the decretals. See *Decretalium Collectiones*, ed. A. Friedberg (Leipzig, 1879: reprint Graz, 1955), 935–936.

Ambrose, Augustine, Guido, and their followers will be considered as Scriptural law not given to all. Yet his teaching will be called catholic or universal, just as the law of grace which contains Scriptural law in itself, as if it had the fullness of knowledge.

Venerable fathers and brothers, I am deeply pained by the ostentation and truly absurd arrogance of this very silly little man, who as ordure from Spain, wishes to be placed above these very holy fathers by his teaching, judgment, foresight, and also piety. What madness, what unbearable shame! According to the saying of Apollo, know yourself and you will not err. For it is a property of folly to recognize the faults of others but to be oblivious to one's own. The preceding is sufficient to show why Guido chose only certain vocables for singing; this choice was made because of its excellence.

Chapter 15

Although there are many inventions in teaching music there is only one in singing it.

Even though the beginning of all arts may be different, yet all of them bring intellectual investigation to one and the same thing, just as many come to the same place through different paths. The teaching of Guido is considered more fitting and clear, and is generally approved for its easiness and brevity. It has been the brilliant teaching of Guido which as a long celebrated example has extended its highest branches throughout the world.

I know and know well that praises can be sung according to the signs of the early Fathers or notes with various names as long as a small semitone is sung either before or after two whole tones, and also by Gregorian letters, just as by Guidonian vocables. One can also sing acceptably by numbers, so that between one and two, as between *ut* and *re,* a whole tone occurs, also between two and three, but between three and four will be a small semitone, moving in this order ad infinitum. Nevertheless, although the beginning of singing had a variety of men, only one and not more is celebrated in music; to think otherwise is the belief of a very foolish man. For what does the prevaricator say, who clearly ventured in his confused treatise to name Odo's music,

Gregory's music, Ambrose's music, and also others? O ignorant, dull, completely insipid and puerile Spaniard! Where did you find this? Through what mental process did you contrive this? For you would have better mentioned the teaching of Gregory or the introduction of Ambrose or others than to speak so ignorantly and ineptly.

Dearest friends, even if the practices of singing are varied, as has been said, and the manner of teaching varied, yet however anyone may sing, he cannot raise or lower a tone unless following the diatonic genus he sings a whole tone or small semitone, a ditone or semiditone, and similar intervals, for the entire study of music revolves about them. So it was necessary to show first by instruction how knowledge of this art can have started in many ways, and then which manner of introducing it is easier and better. Now that this has been discussed every kind of man will acknowledge that God can be praised by the six Guidonian vocables.

Chapter 16

The division of the hand.

Antiquity declared that there were only fifteen letters of the philosophers which expressed every melody of the diatonic genus, namely from the first letter *A* to the third [A]. Anything preceding the first letter or exceeding the third is a repetition of the others. But in the order of the Guidonian hand a division into these parts must be made. The first part is lower, the second median or acute, the third superacute, as this example shows:

Low: A B C D E F G
Median: a b c d e f g
Superacute: a b c d e

The first notes are called low either because they are produced from the bottom of the chest or because they are formed in the first series. The second are acute because they are sung in a higher range. The third are superacute because they are sung in a very high range. In order to bring the understanding of this to you more clearly, I will add the fifteen strings of the philosophers, so that then I may move to an explanation of each.

Chapter 17

Strings of philosophers [according to Capella and Boethius].[44]

Proslambanomenos
Whole tone
Hypate hypaton
Semitone
Parhypate hypaton
Whole tone
Lichanos hypaton. A fourth.
Whole tone
Hypate mesonı
Semitone
Parhypate meson
Whole tone
Lichanos meson
Whole tone
Mese. A fifth; an octave
Whole tone
Paramese. A tritone
Semitone
Trite diezeugmenon
Whole tone
Paranete diezeugmenon
Whole tone
Nete diezeugmenon. A fifth
Semitone
Trite hyperbolaeon
Whole tone
Paranete hyperbolaeon
Whole tone
Nete hyperpolaeon. A disdiapason

44 In Parma *Incun.* 132. The chapter heading is also lacking in the original imprint.

Since above I have given you a description of the fifteen strings of philosophers, now I will proceed to an exposition of each. The Greeks called the first and lowest string proslambanomenos, that is, added or acquired; although it was the last string invented, it was added to the others through necessity. The second is hypate hypaton or lowest of the low which was so named when it was the first string before the existence of proslambanomenos. The third is parhypate hypaton or next to the lowest because it is only a small semitone from the latter. The fourth, lichanos hypaton, is called the index because when it was in the third place, a whole tone from the second string, antiquity plucked the string with the index finger. The fifth, hypate meson, was called the lowest of the median strings, for just as it ends the lowest tones, so it begins the median tones. The sixth, parhypate meson, is next to the lowest of the median tones.

The seventh, lichanos meson, is the index of the median strings in Latin, for the name and word lichanos is chosen from its similarity of position. The eighth is called mese, which is median, because through its position in the middle it is mother and queen of all following terms. The ninth is called paramese, that is, next to mese. The tenth, trite diezeugmenon or the third disjunct string, is at the third place from mese, although it is a small semitone from paramese. The eleventh is called parnete diezeugmenon, that is, next to disjunct nete, which produces the last and highest tone of the disjunct tetrachord. The twelfth is nete diezeugmenon, which is a whole tone from the eleventh and which makes a perfect fifth with mese, the median tone.[45] The thirteenth is trite hyperbolaeon, which is called the third string of the upper and highest tetrachord, for it is higher than its neighboring nete by only a small semitone; although a lowered tone, it is still in the third place above nete. The fourteenth is called paranete hyperbolaeon, that is next to the higher nete, just as paranete diezeugmenon; in the same way it is a whole tone from nete. The fifteenth is called nete hyperbolaeon or the lowest of the upper tetrachord, just as nete diezeugmenon. Let the preceding suffice as a discussion of this matter.

[45] This sentence is lacking in the imprint, and is supplied from a gloss in Parma *Incun. 132.*

Chapter 18

Mutation in song.

Although mutations are considered frivolous and having little meaning by some very intelligent men, in order to satisfy various minds I will treat the subject with brevity, lest in proceeding at greater length I may seem similar to the foolish prevaricator who professes himself to be a musician, when by heavens he is deranged and cut off from the way of truth. For in following Marchettus he has taken up more than four pages in stupid and entirely refutable comments on this subject. For I ask, where is it found? Is it in the school of philosophers from whom every order of consonances emanate? Or is it in Boethius, the leader and monarch of musicians? Does he find it in the pious monk Guido or in Joannes the Carthusian, his eloquent follower? O two-faced Janus, whom no stork bites from behind.[46] Your understanding is futile and you wish praise for it.[47] From where did this hodgepodge come to words.[48] From where this infamous writing?[49] For it is wonderful to be pointed out and proclaimed: He is the one![50] As I said he has followed the crass and inept foolishness of Marchettus as if to offer mackerel and incense in a larger bundle.[51]

O you to whom reason is director and queen, without eyes in the back of your head resist mockery behind your back.[52] For tyros and poor clerics must be taught to produce a whole tone or small semitone according to the necessary letters or vocables, as already stated. With this method I bear witness to its excellence, since they are able to acquire skill in singing in one month, while otherwise they could not do so in three months.

46 Persius, *Satirae,* I, 58. The reference here is to a finger curved in the manner of a stork's bill, which was a gesture of derision.

47 *Ibid.,* I, 84.

48 *Ibid.,* I, 80.

49 *Ibid.*

50 *Ibid.,* I. 28.

51 Cf. *ibid.,* I, 43.

52 *Ibid.,* I, 62.

Mutation[53] is called the change of a name or note if it belongs to the same sound and line and space. It is said further that mutation can occur in any place on the hand where two or three tones have different names, if they are contained in one single letter. On *gamma ut, a re,* and ♮ *mi* no mutation occurs because there is only one vocable. There is also no mutation on ♭ *fa* ♮ *mi.* The reason is that although there are two tones with different names, yet they are not on a single letter. Also they do not belong to one and the same sound; because of the semitone they produce an imperfect sound. These and similar cases are treated by those unintelligent men; such cases undoubtedly have no validity.

Chapter 19

The property of a song.

The property of a song is a certain deduction or exchange of tones arising from a single beginning; the property is changed when its beginning is changed. Note that there are three properties: natural, soft ♭, and square ♮. If a property begins on *c* it is called natural; if on *f* it is sung with soft ♭; and if on *g* with square ♮. From this the common verse arises: *C* gives the natural, *F* soft ♭, and *g* square ♮.

These are the properties of every song. Although they may seem insignificant and banal matters, they have a more rational basis than the other things mentioned above. On account of these three properties three semitones are sung which are different in name but not in interval, as I will explain in the next chapter, notwithstanding the prevaricator's impudence which (as in Cicero's words) is used instead of wisdom.[54]

Chapter 20

The signs of soft ♭ and square ♮.

In the second tract on mixed song we have treated these signs fully, since that is a fitting place. But because the prevaricator's insolence

53 From Marchettus of Padua, *Lucidarium,* in Gerbert, *op. cit.,* III, 90.
54 Cicero, *Epistulae ad Familiares,* I, 10.

and false teaching must be refuted and entirely eradicated, I will include here some things worth knowing about them. Above all it should be kept in mind that the signs of soft♭ and square ♮ are, for boys and for the ignorant, a whole tone or a semitone. Square or hard ♮ is always the key of a small semitone according to the natural and stable order of letters. The sign of soft ♭ is a key or demonstration of a moveable small semitone, and it occurs especially when a tritone must be removed.[55]

For it falls between *f fa ut* and ♭ *fa* ♮ *mi;* it is removed by changing into the third fourth-species, not by virtue of the sign but by virtue of the small semitone. After this danger has been avoided and its sharpness has been turned into a pleasant sound, natural square ♮ must be resumed immediately, that is, by singing according to the aforementioned natural order of letters. For stable semitones, as above in Ch. 8, always fall between *b* and *c*, and *e* and *f*. Moveable semitones are between *a* and round ♭ when a tritone occurs, or in making an imperfect fifth and similar intervals perfect in counterpoint or figural song.

That distinguished man and musician, the Carmelite Joannes Hothby, does not deserve to be despised by you, o prevaricator, who call him idle and without value. As Catullus[56] says, everyone has his own faults assigned to him, but we do not see the bag behind us. For Hothby has named the hard semitone correctly, not because he makes any difference between stable and moveable small semitones, since they are sung with the same amount of breath, but because there is a twofold *b* on ♭ *fa* ♮ *mi,* one signifying a moveable semitone or round ♭, the other a stable semitone or square ♮. According to some the latter is called hard, and therefore he named this semitone hard to show its

[55] The musical examples in Book I are glosses from Parma *Incun. 132* and are not found in the printed edition.

[56] Carmen XXII, 20. An allusion to a fable by Aesop in which we carry a bag or *mantica* in front and in back. The bag in front contains the faults of others and the one in back has our own which we do not see.

difference from the soft semitone or round ♭. So you should keep your tongue in your mouth when you get ready to spew forth something venomous, so that the authority of so many Fathers is not contaminated by your malice.

Let me add this last point: although a tritone may occur frequently in any song, it is regularly in the fifth and sixth mode[57] because of the third fifth-species which arises from a tritone and a small semitone. One must conclude, therefore, that the fifth and sixth mode should be sung with soft ♭ on account of the very frequent appearance of the tritone. This is not always true in the fifth mode, but it occurs especially in the sixth.[58]

Chapter 21

Musical intervals.

Since tropes or modes, which are eight in number, are formed from musical intervals, it seemed more necessary to see what an interval is and how many there are in music before considering modes. An interval is the disposition or arrangement of sounds or tones. Eight are most requisite: whole tone, semitone, ditone, semiditone, tritone, fourth, fifth, and octave.

A whole tone is the complete modulation of the *phthongi* or sounds (for *phthongi* are tones) within appropriate intervals, as *a* and ♮, *c* and *d*, and *d* and *e*, singing the letters in order. Likewise in the Guidonian vocables the interval falls between *ut re, re mi, fa sol,* and *sol la.* I will show you an example in a progression of letters when note shapes are lacking through the fault of the printers. I had collected many examples in notation, especially on counterpoint and mensural music, whose omission I strongly regret, particularly because of some ambiguous cases which are not easily understood except by some illustrative sign or example. For this reason, if the original of this work ever comes to your hands, you will be able to understand very clearly by sight and mind what is uncertain. Now we must show of what parts a whole tone is made.

57 Burtius uses *tonus* for *modus* in this chapter.
58 This sentence is a gloss in Parma *Incun. 132.*

According to Boethius [59] a whole tone consists of two semitones, namely a small and large semitone which is an apotome. This contains a small semitone and a comma. The meaning of a comma is: if two semitones are removed from a whole tone, a comma remains. For greater understanding let me propose a more detailed approach in order to learn thoroughly the work of both ancient and modern writers. A diesis is one half of a semitone, and according to some, a comma is one half a diesis. But in Bk. III [60] of *Musica* our Boethius shows rationally that a comma excedes one half a diesis. He also states that Philolaus measured smaller parts. Note that a diesis and a comma cannot be produced by the human voice, nor also the smaller intervals, the schisma and diaschisma. The schisma is one half a comma and the diaschisma is a half of a diesis, that is, one half of a small semitone.

Although it is clear that a small semitone is not equal to a large semitone, and a sesquioctave proportion cannot be divided equally with similar superparticular intervals, yet I believe it should be discussed in a further explanation that a whole tone seems to be equally divisible. For a whole tone contains two small semitones and a comma, as previously stated. Thus a complete half of a whole tone arises from two diaschismas which form a small semitone and a schisma or one half a comma. So it is correctly stated that a complete half of a whole tone can be divided into two diaschismas and one schisma. From this it is ascertained that a complete semitone, that is, an equal division of a whole tone, seems to differ from a small semitone by one schisma. But an apotome differs from a small semitone by two schismas or one comma. For two schismas complete one comma as mentioned above. So a small semitone contains two dieses and a large semitone also has two plus a comma. It follows from this that a whole tone is completed by four dieses and a comma. To illustrate this I will present six letters and five intervals in this order:

A diesis B diesis C diesis D diesis E comma F

Small semitone - - - - Large semitone - - - - - -

[59] *Op. cit.*, III, 6; p.277 in Friedlein edition.

[60] *Loc. cit.*

Enough has been said about the whole tone. Note that according to Guido *tonus* is named for *tonandus,* because it sounds perfectly from pitch to pitch and refers to a single interval. But an interval is called the distance between a high and low sound or the space between one tone and another.

A small semitone is also the distance or interval of two sounds. It is not a complete tone, for according to Gregorian letters it is found between ♮ *c, e f,* and *a* ♭ when a tritone occurs. In Guidonian syllables a small semitone always falls between *mi fa* in ascending and descending. It is not called a semitone because semi means half, as some say, but because it is not a complete tone on account of the comma, for it is not one half of a whole tone but the smallest of its two parts.

A ditone is the union of three pitch names and two whole tones, as low *G B*, low *c e,*[61] etc. In Guidonian vocables it falls between *ut mi* and *fa la.* It has only two species, as you see, and is named from the Greek *dia,* which means *duo* in Latin, since it occupies two whole tones.

A semiditone is also a union of three pitch names or a whole tone and a small semitone. It is named from semi, as a semitone, and ditone, an imperfect ditone. It lies between low *d f*, low *e g,* etc. In Guidonian vocables it is between *re fa* and *mi sol.* As you see, it has only two species.

A tritone is a very discordant aggregation of four pitch names and three whole tones. It is named from *tris* or *tres* and *tonus* because it is made up of three successive whole tones. It regularly lies between *f* and square ♮ ; in Guidonian vocables it sounds an upward *fa mi* with three steps in between, and *mi fa* downward with three intermediary steps. Note that whenever this occurs it should be changed to the third fourth-species or *ut fa* in vocables. But especially in a rising or descending fifth the interval is sung as noted above in the third fifth-species.[62]

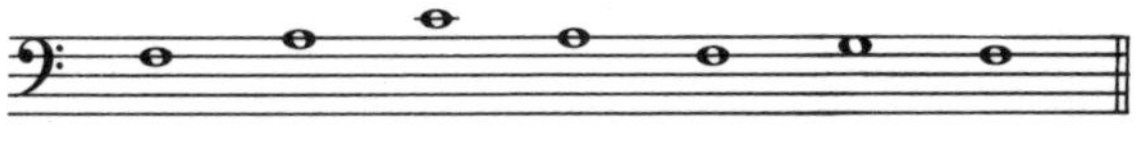

61 Burtius has *G A, c d.*

62 This sentence and the example are in a gloss of Parma *Incun. 132.* The musical illustration in G. Massera, *Florum Libellus* (Florence, 1975), p. 94, ftn., 122, is inaccurate.

A fourth or diatessaron is a union of four pitch-names or two whole tones and one small semitone. It is named from *dia,* which is *de* or *per,* and *tessera* or four, since it is made up of four sounds. It has three species, the first beween low *A d,* the second between ♮ *e,* and the third between *C F.* Or the first lies between low *D G,* the second beween low *E* and high *A,* and the third between low *G* and high *C.* In the Guidonian vocables the first is *re sol,* the second *mi la,* and the third *ut fa.*

A perfect fifth or diapente is a connection of five tones or three whole tones and one small semitone. It is named from *dia* in Greek, which is *de* or *per,* and *pente,* which consists of five tones. It has four species. The first lies between low *d* and high *a*, the second between low *E* and high ♮ , the third between low *F* and high *C*, and the fourth between low *g* and high *d*. The Guidonian vocables are first *re la,* second *mi mi,* third *fa fa,* and fourth *ut sol.* The imperfect fifth will be treated fully in the tract on counterpoint. It lies naturally between ♮ *mi* and *F fa ut;* how it

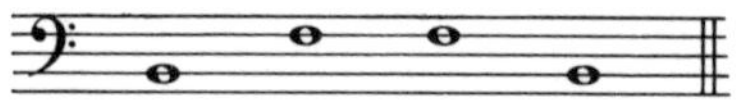

should be made perfect is well known.

Chapter 22

The octave and its praises.

The octave is the most perfect of the three simple consonances. If[63] I had a hundred tongues, a hundred mouths, and a voice of iron, I could never give it sufficient praise. The philosopher has celebrated its praises at length, and especially in Problems XIX, 18.[64] What about Boethius, Guido, and other musicians? Did they not extol it with highest praises? As recounted above, Pliny in Bk. II of *Historia Naturalis* said it filled

63 Vergil, *Georgics* II, 43.
64 *Burtius has Problems* XXIX, 18.

the entire universe when he spoke about the heavens, for it extends from earth to signifer or the heavenly constellations. It is sweet, pleasant, concordant, and cheerful, for it is formed in unity and equality. This is simple or duple or multiple; not only is it never discordant, but it produces one and the same very pleasant sound.

What else shall I say? An octave is formed from a fourth and a fifth. It contains all the preceding intervals, and as a good mother, cherishes and nourishes them in her bosom. In this way an octave is called a diapason, for *pan* means all, since it contains the entire concordant universe. So Cicero says in *Somnium Scipionis:*[65] The eight spheres in which the motion of the modes is the same, produce seven different intervals; this number is the key to almost everything, for learned men devoted to string instruments and song have shown that it returns to its origin.

An octave consists of eight sounds or five whole tones and two small semitones. It has as many species as there are Gregorian letters. If you begin on the Greek gamma you will have eight, but from low *a* to low *g* there are only seven. Without question seven disdiapasons can also be formed just as the seven octaves.[66] If you connect a fifth to an octave, a twelfth will result, and if you double an octave it is called a disdiapason. Its ratio will be seen when we discuss proportions. A diagram of the octave-species follows.

[65] *De Re Publica,* VI, 18, 18. Burtius's text of this celebrated passage differs somewhat from the one presently accepted.

[66] For a diagram of the seven disdiapasons see Gallicus, in Coussemaker, *op. cit.,* IV, 340.

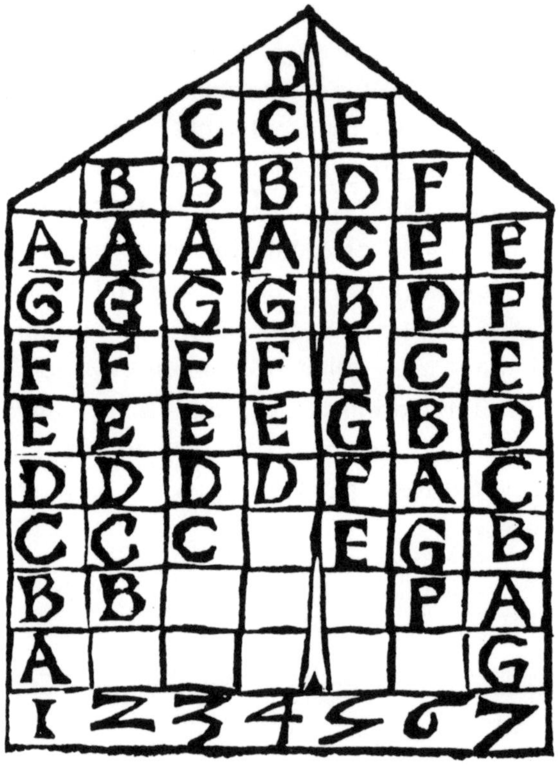

Chapter 23

Ancient tropes, tones, or modes changed into four authentic and four plagal modes.

The Greeks had seven tropes named from various territories. First was Hypodorian, second Hypophrygian, third Hypolydian, fourth Dorian, fifth Phrygian, sixth Lydian, seventh Mixolydian; the eighth was Hypermixolydian formed by Ptolemy, who was a distinguished musician among his contemporaries. In the same way after the coming of Christ, there were only four modes or Tones in the early Church. The first is protus or *primus* in Latin, the second deuterus or *secundus,* the third tritus or *tertius* from *tris* or *tres*, and finally the fourth tetrardus or *quartus* from *tetra* or four.

The four modes have individual tonics. The first is on low *d*, the second on low *e*, the third on low *f*, and the fourth on low *g*. These letters are called finals by church musicians, since every song composed according to Gregorian rule ends on one of them. The modern authentic and plagal modes also end in this way, as will be seen later. According to their finals the above tropes can have a fourth or four vocables below and an octave above, in which case they are perfect; lacking this range they are imperfect and curtailed. If they exceed this range a little they are not superfluous as the prevaricator says, but are called pluperfect according to the authority of Johannes the Carthusian and others. But keeping in mind the opinion of Cicero that a high-pitched cry hurts the voice and throat, the modes are brought into a median range by dividing them into authentic and plagal parts.

The first are called authentic because they rise or because they have greater authority. They are said to ascend to the octave, but according to Guidonian rules they can descend one tone below the final. Note that I said "can", for it is one thing to say "can" and another to say "must", just as one may say that if they do not descend one note below the final, they are still perfect. This follows the formulas of Joannes the Carthusian.

The second are called plagal, as if subjugate or lateral, because they are, as it were, servants under the power of the authentic modes. All plagal modes are considered to ascend to the fifth above the final, and sometimes the sixth; they descend a fourth below the final, or a fifth according to some. The rules governing them are the same as those I noted above. The first modes are uneven numbers, or first, third, fifth, and seventh. Plagal modes are even, or second, fourth, sixth, and eighth. I will present concisely the formulas of all, and first the authentic modes.

Formula of the first authentic.[67]

$C\ ^{t}D\ ^{t}E\ ^{s}F\ ^{t}G\ ^{t}A\ ^{t}\natural\ ^{s}C\ ^{t}D$

Final

This is the formula of the first authentic formed within the fourth octave-species and arising from the first fifth- and fourth-species. Its

67 t = whole tone and s = semitone.

usual incipits are on *c*, as *O beatum pontificem;* on *d*, in which incipit and final are the same, as *Ecce nomen domini;* on *e*, although rarely, as *Gaudete in domino;* on *f*, as *Ipsi soli;* and on *g*, as *Canite tuba* etc.

Formula of the second authentic

D ᵗ *E* ˢ *F* ᵗ *G* ᵗ *A* ᵗ ♮ ˢ *C* ᵗ *D* ᵗ *E*
Final

This is the formula of the second authentic formed within the fifth octave-species and arising from the second fifth- and fourth-species. Its usual incipits are on *e*, as *Quando natus es*, in *f*, as *Nunc scio vere*, on *g*, as *Multa Quidem*, and on *a*, as *Tertia dies est*, etc.

Formula of the third authentic

F ᵗ *G* ᵗ *A* ᵗ ♮ ˢ *C* ᵗ *D* ᵗ *E* ˢ *F*
Final

This is the formula of the third authentic formed within the sixth octave-species and arising from the third fifth- and fourth species. Its usual incipits are on *e*, as *Haurietis aquas*, on *g* but rarely, as *Non vos relinquam*, in *a*, as *Quinque prudentes*, and on *c*, as *Ecce dominus veniet*.

Formula of the fourth authentic

F ᵗ *G* ᵗ *A* ᵗ ♮ ˢ *C* ᵗ *D* ᵗ *E* ˢ *F* ᵗ *G*
Final

This is the formula of the fourth authentic formed within the seventh octave-species and arising from the fourth fifth- and first fourth-species. Its usual incipits are: on *f* you hardly find any examples, on *g* is *Assumpta est Maria*, on *a* it is rare, as the Communion *Domus mea*, [68] on ♮ , as *Dixit Dominus*, on *c*, as *Benedicta*, and on *d*, as *Sit nomen Domini*. The first formula of the plagal follows.

68 Massera, *Florum Libellus*, p. 100, has *Communio domus mea. Domus mea* is the Communion chant in the Mass for the Dedication of a Church.

Formula of the first plagal

Γ A ♮ C D E F G A B
Final

This is the formula of the first plagal within the first octave-species but formed from the first fifth- and fourth-species. Its incipits are on *a,* as *Omnes patriarchae,* on *c,* as *Nonne cor nostrum,* on *d,* as *Ecce in nubibus,* and on *f,* as *Quem vidistis.* You very rarely find examples on other pitches.

Formula of the second plagal

A t ♮ s *C* t *D* t *E* s *F* t *G* t *A* t ♮ s *C*

This is the formula of the second plagal within the second octave-species but having the interval of the fourth below the fifth. Its incipits are found on *c*, as *Homo erat in Hierusalem,* on *d*, as *Prope esto Domine* and *Benedicta tu,* on *e*, as *Gaude Maria virgo,* on *f*, as *Recessit igitur,* on *g,* as *O mors ero,*[69] and on *a* in the same way that the fourth and third plagal differ.

Formula of the third plagal

C t *D* t *E* s *F* t *G* t *A* s *B* t *C* t *D*
Final

This is the formula of the third plagal formed within the third octave-species but having the fourth below the fifth. Its incipits are scarcely different than those of the fifth mode or third authentic, but they may begin on the final, as *Verbum caro,* or on the fourth, as *Si ego verus Christi discipulus.* Yet there is a great difference between them. When a song does not descend into the sixth mode,as it is properly called in the order of modes, or reach the height of the fifth mode, but begins on the tenth and frequently repeats the eleventh, then it belongs to the fifth mode. If it only ascends to the ninth it will belong to the sixth mode. Let this be enough on their recognition.

69 Massera, *op. cit.,* p. 101, has here: *O mors; eraro* in *a. O mors ero* is the beginning of an antiphon sung at Lauds on Holy Saturday.

Formula of the fourth plagal

$C^{t}\ D^{t}\ E^{s}\ F^{t}\ G^{t}\ A^{t}\ ♮^{s}\ C^{t}\ D^{t}\ E$
Final

This is the formula of the fourth plagal or eighth mode formed within the fourth octave-species and having a fourth below the fifth. Its incipits are on *c*, as *Ecce ancilla Domini,* on *a*, as *Complecti sunt,* on *g*, as *In illa die,* on *f*, as *Hodie Maria,* and on *d*, as *Virgines Domini.* The eighth mode is different than the seventh mode because the eighth has a third, fourth, and fifth, which the seventh does not have. The seventh has a thirteenth and fourteenth which the eighth does not have.

Chapter 24

Antiphons or plainsong with small ranges.

After showing the varieties of authentic and plagal modes I will treat concisely antiphons or songs with small ranges. It should be known first that an authentic song in this very narrow range rarely exceeds a fifth, and a plagal rarely exceeds a fourth. Authentic examples are the antiphons *Dabit ei Dominus, Caelum et terram transibunt, Clamor meus,* and others. Plagal examples are the antiphon *Da nobis Domine* and other similar songs.

Chapter 25

The difference between authentic and plagal antiphons according to their final saeculorum or euouae.

Although antiphons with a narrow range are differentiated in the same natural way as other plainchant, since sometimes they can hardly be distinguished, they are treated here for the understanding of practitioners, not of musicians. The latter undoubtedly have complete knowledge of this subject.

I will describe briefly some rules for differentiating all such modes, as here: Every antiphon ending on low *d* and beginning its *saeculorum* or *euouae* on high *a*, with an ambitus of *re la,* undoubtedly is in the first authentic mode, as the antiphon *Primum quaerite regnum Dei* and similar ones. Note that the first authentic mode has twelve *differentiae,* as is very clear in an antiphonary. Every antiphon ending on low *d* with a *saeculorum* on low *f* and a range of *re fa,* undoubtedly is in the second mode. This belongs to the first plagal; it is second in the order of modes and has one *differentia.*

Every antiphon ending on low *e* with an *euouae* or *saeculorum* on high *c* [70] and a range of *mi fa,* truly belongs to the third mode and has five *differentiae.* Every antiphon ending on low *e* with a *saeculorum* on high *a* and a range of *mi la,* undoubtedly belongs to the fourth mode and has three *differentiae.*

Every antiphon ending on low *f* with a *saeculorum* on high *c* and a range of *fa fa,* belongs to the authentic fifth mode and has one *differentia.* Every antiphon ending on low *f* with its *euouae* ending on high *a* and a range of *fa la,* belongs to the plagal sixth mode and has one *differentia.*

Every antiphon ending on low *g* with its *saeculorum* on high *d* and a range of *ut sol* belongs to the authentic seventh mode and has six *differentiae.* Every antiphon ending on low *g* with its *euouae* or *saeculorum* on high *c* and a range of *ut fa,* belongs to the plagal eighth mode and has five *differentiae.* The antiphon *In exitu Israel* with its *differentiae*, although not rising at the end up to a fourth, undoubtedly belongs to the plagal eighth tone, especially when it ends on low *g.* Its beginning and ending should not be a cause for wonder, because similar changes can be made by musicians and with ecclesiastical permission can be publically promulgated. This is according to the authority of Joannes the Carthusian.

70 Burtius has high *e.*

Chapter 26

Antiphons that end irregularly on A in modern practice.

Three *differentiae* ending on high *a* are found among church musicians, and the moderns call them irregular on account of the pitch of the final letter. Since some question whether the fourth, sixth, or another mode is their basis, I believe this should be answered. Since their antiphons, namely *Dominus regit me, Sicut myrrha,* and *Factus sum* with the antiphon *Benedicta tu* and others are plagal, they are considered to belong to the fourth mode rather than any other because of the fourth they have below and because of their conformity in incipits and finals. So it is concluded that when an antiphon ending on high *a* has an *euouae* ending on high *d*, then it belongs to the fourth mode. This is the common opinion of musicians, although some venture to call them mixed, that is, as remote from their own fourth- and fifth-species as from others. They give as examples the antiphons *Stetit angelus* and *Servi Domini,* which seem to be similar in sound and species of consonances. But on this, o reader, make your judgment so that reason is the ruler and the mind obeys. After considering the above connections the same decision should be reached concerning finals on ♮ or on high *c*.

Chapter 27

How to begin psalms in each mode.

The first and sixth mode begin on *F G A* or *fa sol la* in vocables. The second, third, and eighth begin on *ut re fa,* the fourth on *la sol la,* and the fifth on *ut mi sol.* The seventh begins on *sol fa sol.* Psalms ending on *a* begin on high *d c d.*

Chapter 28

Who first brought a proper moderation to tropes or modes and made them renowned.

Dearest friends, now that various considerations and differences of all tropes have been examined, I will explain in detail who developed such a kind of music and made it illustrious. Before St. Gregory we find various plainsong codices written with different characters of ciphers, so to speak, as stated at the beginning of this book. Some were episcopal and others were songs by some individual. This has been shown in the testimony of Guido, who flourished in Italy after Boethius and other ancient musicians. Being under great obligation to him I cannot name him with sufficient praise. Although he is worthy of perpetual honor and praise he was not first to play the cithara or organ. Nor did the early philosophers or Boethius or any of the musicians renowned for a long time have the honor of bringing together and developing from these tropes such a mellifluous and sweet concord of melody.

The reader should not wonder if first I may have described the eight modes of the Greeks. This I testify is true, but you will not find that they are distinguished by such a beautifully soaring and receding melody. For[71] if you consider this correctly it is clearly extraordinary that in nocturnal responsories the melody seems to stimulate lethargic and indifferent somnolents to vigilance. In antiphons it sounds clearly and smoothly, but in introits, as if by the voice of a crier, we are called to the divine Office. In tracts and graduals it sounds clearly and at length; it seems to inspire us with its humble tone. The same thing is evident in offertories with their verses and especially in communions, according as moderation in this art allows. In these chants there is every kind of rise, fall, and repetition of tones that is delightful to the connoisseur and fatiguing to the learner, and also a truly wonderful departure from other songs.

So that the minds of readers do not become fatigued by a verbose discussion, I will ask, who was there to clearly define this art? Was he perhaps from Gaul since Gaul is the mother of singers, or from England or all Britain? Was he German, Iberian, Saboean, or someone known in all these places so far removed from barbarians? Did he come from Spain? For according to Solinus,[72] Spain not only abounded in every-

[71] The rest of the paragraph is based on the *Dialogus de musica* by Odo (?) in Gerbert, *op. cit.*, I, 276.

[72] *Collectanea*, Ch.35.

thing material that was costly or necessary to existence, but also was illustrious through the wonderful talents of its men. Pliny and Pomponius Mela testify to this. Where are the two Senecas, where the teaching of the most eloquent Lucan? Thus Martial says to Licianus: Eloquent Corduba extols the two Senecas and the peerless Lucan. Jocose Gades rejoices in her Canius, Emertia in my Decianus. In you, Licianus, our Bilbilis will glory, nor be silent about me.[73] Yet among barbarous nations distinguished and outstanding talents were conspicuous. I say barbarous because countries beyond the Roman empire are called barbarous nations; as regards laws, if I remember correctly, this is stated in a gloss in the preface.[74]

But all these nations, as proven by very efficacious testimony, have received an undiminished source and increase of learning in Italy, the mother and sustainer of the entire earth. According to Pliny in Book 3 of *Historia Naturalis,* Italy is the homeland, parent, and support of the whole world; chosen by divine will it made heaven itself more brilliant. It unified scattered power, enlightened customs and brought the discordant and hard languages of so many peoples into communication with a common tongue. In short, it gave humanity to man and became the home of all peoples on earth.

Then there is the completely vital and unfailing moderation of health-giving skies, such fertile fields, sunny hills, shady meadows, generous varieties of forests, abundance of mountains, and fruitfulness of olive trees. There are so many fine herds of sheep and oxen, so many lakes, rivers, and springs giving water everywhere, so many ports and harbors open the world's commerce and, as it were, extending into the open sea for the benefit of man. And I do not mention the talents, customs, and people subdued in arms and in their language.

The Greeks, very widespread during the time of their glory, laid claim to part of the country and called it Magna Graecia or lower Italy. As Pliny says in his last book, it was very illustrious in its men and women, outstanding in its leaders, military might, and talented men. What else shall I say? For the truth cannot hide itself. What about Cicero, most eloquent of men? He not only excelled in philosophy but

73 *Epigrams,* I, 61.

74 See the preface of Justinian's *Institutionum* in *Corpus Iuris Civilis,* vol. I, Berlin, 1954.

was distinguished in the knowledge of all liberal arts. That music was renowned among them is seen in his written works, especially in the book on the dream of Scipio and in *De Universo.* In the beginning of *Tusculanae,* where he states he wanted to relate that the Greeks excelled in all mathematics, namely music, geometry, and arithmetic, he says: but we have defined the character of this art by examining its usefulness with measure and reason.

What about the integrity, dignity, and severity of Cato? What of Camillus, Fabricius, Marcellus, the Scipio family? Or as Valerius says, the best part of heaven, the divine Caesars? I will not omit the very terse eloquence of Sallust, for he, a product of learned men, was the first Crispus[75] in Roman history. What about the remarkable Livy who, in the words of Martial, recorded so many Roman deeds in such an immense volume? Or Valerius Maximus, who set down with the greatest care in the chapters of his books the lives and customs of men, both domestic and foreign? He approaches the enormous volume of Pliny, in which from varied opinions Pliny described the movement of the universe, what is understandable in it, and the differing natures of men, events, and animals.

Did not the chief pontiffs and legislators arise from Italy? What about Maro, who as if a star in the firmament, is a unique ideal? Or Ovid and Propertius, distinguished poets? Or the eloquence of the very deserving Tibullus, Catullus, and Stella? What about the works of Statius and Silius Italicus, or Horace, Juvenal, and Persius with his very concise books of satires? For the sake of brevity I omit those men of Italy in our times who have gradually emerged and distinguished themselves. They are jewels, a union of sapphires and other precious stones which Italy brings forth and develops. So let the frenzy of the ignorant be silenced and let them give up their unbridled impudence; they should examine all the distinguished talents Italy has given us, not without the highest praise for everyone.

With reason Italy is indebted to St. Gregory, who made that country illustrious by his sanctity, teaching, and works. He was born in Rome and became prefect of the city. Not only did he write forty homilies on

75 The surname of Sallust, the Roman historian.

the Gospels, thirty-five on Job, twenty on Ezechiel, a book on pastoral care and four books of dialogs, but he also handed down to the Catholic church what I have called tropes, which he disseminated with such proper moderation that they are still used at present. Do not believe that this is my opinion, but it is Guido's whose words I use. The [76] very saintly Gregory, whose precepts the Church observes very carefully in all matters, handed down to the Church a wonderfully composed antiphonary and through his own labor gave it to his disciples. Since it is not read anywhere that he learned this art through wordly knowledge, it is very surely established that he received a fullness of knowledge under divine guidance. So it was evident that this kind of music, given to St. Gregory by divine inspiration, is supported not only by human but also divine authority. This is Guido's opinion in Book 3 of his *Musica.*

If you consider well what was in question it is clear that it has now been fully revealed. Let the malice of the repudiator be removed, as he does not wish confidence attributed to so great a man. Unless a man is distinguished and completely holy, nothing emerges from him. Eusebius in his *Chronicle* and others have described this. I consider it truly should be believed and retained. From the preceding discussion the reader not only has an answer to his query but also has collected many valuable ideas about the praise of Italy.

Chapter 29

What is necessary for those wishing to apply angelic song or plain song to sacred music.

As I had promised I have assembled in this short tract anything that can be understood about angelic song, or plain song, as it is called. For those wishing to easily understand antiphons, responsories, hymns, and similar plainchant, and who also wish to create new and very devout songs of their own, the way is undoubtedly very clearly open to them. Just as it is necessary for teachers in the course of their studies

[76] This passage, comprising the remainder of the paragraph, occurs in Odo's (?) *Dialogus de musica,* in Gerbert, *op. cit.,* I, 275.

to have read thoroughly the books of learned men and many of the ancients they wish to follow, so also it is necessary that those wishing to put plainchant to sacred words have frequented churches a long time, singing from sacred books. They should also know about the genera, kinds of consonances, constitutions, modes, and tropes or tones already treated before this. You can follow this material if you have read thoroughly our introduction containing the principal information, and if you have given the proper form to each trope or mode. According to Guido a trope is a kind of song which is also called a mode. Let me add this final point, that we understand and follow the Gregorian style with all the strength of our minds. For as Guido says, whoever neglects completely the home of St. Gregory for the sake of the songs of others opposes the highest ecclesiastical authority.

Chapter 30

The conservation of the voice and how it should be guarded in singing.

Although earlier in Ch. 8 the voice was fully treated, in this last part of the first tract I would like to speak about its conservation and the carefulness with which it should be used in singing. In order to preserve the human voice three things are necessary and appropriate. First, in beginning a song one should not produce a very powerful breath or too high a tone, but the opening of songs should employ a moderate amount of breath and a low tone, for otherwise, according, to Cicero in Bk. 3 of *Rhetorica,* the windpipe is hurt and the lungs are overburdened. The opposite, according to Albert Magnus,[77] helps and supports the movement of air to the voice, just as in a pair of bellows. Thus moderation must be used so that we do not begin on too high or too low a pitch, for a high-pitched outcry injures the throat and voice and also disturbs the listener, as Cicero states. If we begin a little lower, gradually the throat and windpipe warm up and fill with air; then the tone which is produced in various ways, is led into a certain even and constant sound.

[77] *Op. cit.,* vol. VII, *pars* I, Book 2, Tract 3, Ch. 22.

The second necessity is to make use of appropriate exercise. For in a remarkable way exercise contributes to clearing and preserving the voice. Celsus says that the result of exercise is sweat and exercise should be taken before eating.[78] If the body has lost its health, which is established mostly by exercise, it is inevitable that the voice will not remain clear and pure, but will become totally weakened and damaged. A well adjusted man, as Celsus says,[79] is healthy and his own master. He should have variety in his life, now in the country, now in the city, often in the fields, at sea, hunting, resting sometimes but more often exercising. Inactivity weakens the body, labor strengthens it; inactivity produces senility, labor a long youth. Thus it can truly be understood that exercise is no little help to health.

We read in *De studio et industria,* Bk. 4,[80] by Valerius, that because of exceedingly poor hearing, Demosthenes by continuous exercise brought his voice to a mature and pleasing sound; also being afflicted with weak lungs, he changed through labor what bodily misfortune had denied him, so that he spoke many lines in a single breath and enunciated them at a rapid pace. Standing on the seashore he orated to the crash of opposing waves so that for practice he applied with strengthened ears the patient use of powerful speeches to this noise. What shall I say about the pebbles he put in his mouth to free his tongue? He was accustomed to speak where there was a free and open space. As Valerius says, he fought with natural phenomena. He emerged the victor, overcoming adversity by the very tenacious strength of his mind. Cicero has stated the same thing in Bk. 5 of *De finibus bonorum et malorum*. So you who tend to weakness can strengthen your voice and determination by his example, and can sustain them with the very powerful strength of his energy.

The third and last necessity in conserving the voice is to avoid extremes in food and drink. For the philosopher[81] says in Bk. 2 of *Ethics* that just as an excess or a lack of work corrupts a man, so too much or too little food and drink ruins his health. But moderation

78 Celsus, *De medicina,* I, 2.
79 *Ibid.,* I, 1.
80 VIII, 4, 1.
81 Aristotle.

increases and preserves it. In this way he brings together what applies to the well-being of man. For nothing is as pleasant as food well cooked and digested, nothing affects health and acuteness of the senses more, and nothing helps illness as much as moderate refreshment. A sufficient amount of nourishment produces both health and pleasure, but an abundance causes disorders and troubles and general illnesses. Thus moderation in everything must be observed; according to Martial, we approve what is moderate and between the extremes. Therefore let us choose wholesome foods, easy to digest and conducive to good temperaments. Beware of rough foods hard to digest, for they create bad temperaments. Concerning all this see Cornelius Celsus, Bk. 2, Ch. 17,[82] *De Medicina.* As a means of sustenance food and drink may be very nutritive, moderately so, or less nutritious.

Among drinks there are three kinds of wine, as Pliny says in Bk. 14, namely, dry, sweet, and diluted. Dry wine is superior, sweet wine is less fragrant, and diluted wine is more fragrant. They are divided according to the ages of the singers. According to Celsus, Bk. 1,[83] *De Medicina,* diluted wine must be given to boys, as it is very mild, and undiluted wine, that is, without water, to men of middle age, because it may disturb the emotions. Wine diluted with water is a very useful drink, as in Pliny, Bk. 3 and Bk. 20 of *Historia Naturalis.* But undiluted wine should be drunk especially in winter time, although the rule of a clear mind for man, free of inebriation, must be adhered to and observed.

Let me add one thing more: that clerics must abstain wholeheartedly from every unlawful pleasure, for inordinate pleasure is fearful because it conquers even the holy. According to Martial there is no one of such tender and constant modesty who may not engage in unnatural vice or relations with a woman.[84] Highly dangerous are summer and autumn because it is not beneficial then, as Celsus[85] says. Although it is more tolerable in autumn, if possible one should abstain totally in summer. Concerning what is practical in winter, the following concerns not the

82 Actually Ch. 18.

83 Ch. 3.

84 *Epigrams,* XI, 45.

85 *Op. cit.,* I, 3. Here Burtius paraphrases Celsus who said: *Neque aestate vero, neque autumno utilis venus est.*

religious but married persons. Too frequent coitus debilitates and enervates the body, and completely ruins the voice. So Juvenal [86] says: They are the women who inhibit the ability of Chrysogonus to sing.

These points have been adduced for the conservation of the voice; without them no consonance can be expressed. Now I come to the second tract, from which you will savor completely the mellifluous harmony of consonances if constant solicitude and pleasure in study will take hold.

Book II by Nicolaus Burtius of Parma, containing the rules of mixed song or counterpoint.

Following Lactantius,[87] I think that for a sagacious man there is no sweeter food for thought than the knowledge of truth. Although in the writings of many singers on this discipline some things have been unnecessary and useless, others have been published that are brilliant and worthy of study. Having removed the superfluous by truth and by examining the material, let me briefly bring everything together.

Since counterpoint is the key to learning mensural or figural song, as they say, first and foremost we will teach what counterpoint is and why it has the name. For anyone who would learn about mensural music without counterpoint will always remain in darkness, as it is said. Secondly, by adding some rules of early writers we will easily show the way to how many consonances are perfect and how many are imperfect, and then how they are arranged in song. Let us get to the subject.

Counterpoint is nothing else but simple song in a certain way dupled or tripled and so on ad infinitum.[88] Or it is the moderator of consonances and dissonances. Counterpoint is named from a very common way of speaking, from *con* or "together with" and *pongo, gis,* or tones sounding at the same time. It is properly called mixed song, that is, composed of perfect and imperfect intervals. Likewise figural song is a certain breaking up or lightening of the voices from the severity of counterpoint.

86 *Satires,* VI, 73.
87 *Institutiones divinae,* I, 1, 20.
88 From Gallicus, in Coussemaker, *op. cit.,* IX, 383.

Chapter 1

Perfect and imperfect consonances

Counterpoint begins and ends with only two perfect consonances, the fifth and octave; two are imperfect consonances, as a ditone and a fifth with a whole tone, which forms a hexachord, usually called a sixth by singers. Other intervals are combinations of these, as a twelfth, a disdiapason, and similar intervals. But in order to give a clearer understanding to many clerics, I will present without ambiguity a rather common explanation of the subject.

In music there are nine concords: unison, third, fifth, sixth, octave, tenth, twelfth,[89] thirteenth, and fifteenth. Of these five are perfect and four are imperfect. Perfect intervals are the unison, fifth, octave, twelfth, and fifteenth. Imperfect intervals are the third, sixth, tenth, and thirteenth. Note that although we call the unison a consonance, it is not properly a consonance as the ordinary singer believes, but the origin of consonances. For a consonance is a concordant and pleasing mixture of a high and low sound, while a unison does not contain these parts. Also, just as a monad in arithmetic is not a number but the origin of numbers, so a unison in music is not considered a consonance. When we are on a unison we do not dissonate or sing discant, but we produce a unison, as this example clearly shows.[90]

The unison, placed at the beginning, is the origin and basis of all other intervals, as it were; in this way the disdiapason is reached. Among all these intervals you see some are unisons, some not, some equisonant, some consonant, and some *emelles*. Unisons are those which when struck produce one and the same sound. Their sound is either high or low, as the first string of this example shows. Intervals with a lower and higher sound are not unisons.

Equisonant intervals are those which when struck together form in a certain way a simple sound from two sounds, as an octave and a disdiapason. Consonant intervals are those which make a composite, mixed, and sweet sound, as a fifth and a twelfth. *Emelles* intervals are

[89] The interval of a twelfth was omitted from the list.

[90] No illustration was printed. See the illustration at the end of this chapter.

those which, although not consonant, are appropriate to counterpoint, as a ditone, semiditone, major sixth, major tenth, etc. By some they are called compatible dissonances. Intervals not appropriate to music are incompatible, as a fourth, seventh, ninth, eleventh, etc. They are also called *exmelles,* that is, removed from every musical pleasantness. This is a description of perfect and imperfect consonances. Now we will see how they are arranged in practice.

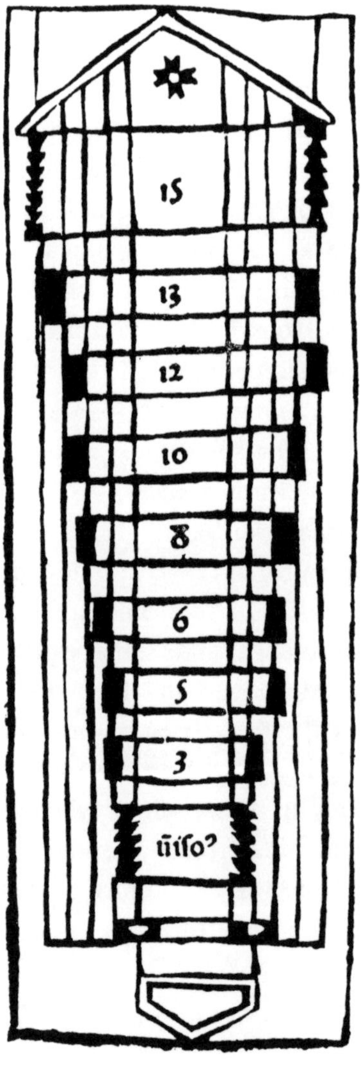

Chapter 2

How[91] *perfect consonances and compatible dissonances are arranged in practice.*

A unison, the origin and basis of the above consonances, regularly has a ditone following it. A ditone or major third, as our singers say, moves to a fifth. A semiditone or minor third, since it contains a small semitone, seeks a unison, and thus should be considered the opposite, although sometimes it can move to a fifth, especially when it is given the sign of a diesis or a coniuncta is interposed, for then it becomes a major third. These[92] compatible dissonances are produced within a fifth, just as a child in its mother's womb, and consequently they move toward that interval.

Also, a whole tone with a fifth or a major sixth, seeks an octave, just as a tenth seeks a twelfth and a thirteenth a fifteenth; this was shown in the preceding example. So it is clear that these compatible dissonances have their own parent and mother to whom they are appropriately subject.

Chapter 3

Five precepts to be observed in counterpoint.

First precept

Counterpoint must never begin or end on compatible dissonances.[93] The reason is that they make a somewhat uncertain concord with which the sense of hearing is pleased, yet the mind only has repose in the nature of a perfect interval. Thus counterpoint begins and ends on perfect consonances, although the penultimate interval may be a compatible dissonance. For example, if the tenor has *d, f, g, a, f, e, d*, or *re, fa, sol,*

[91] Burtius' *Tractatus pulcher.* MS II 785, ff. 41v – 44r, in the Bibliothèque Royale of Brussels, begins here.

[92] From Gallicus, in Coussemaker, *op. cit.* IV, 394.

[93] From Gallicus, in Coussemaker, *op. cit.*, IV, 394, Other precepts also derive from Gallicus.

la, fa, mi, re, then the discant will begin on high *a la,* the fifth, or on high *d,* which is *sol* and a perfect octave, or on other perfect consonances; beginning on *d* the discant will be *d, c,* ♮ , *a, d, c, d,* or *sol, fa, mi, re, sol, fa, sol.*[94]

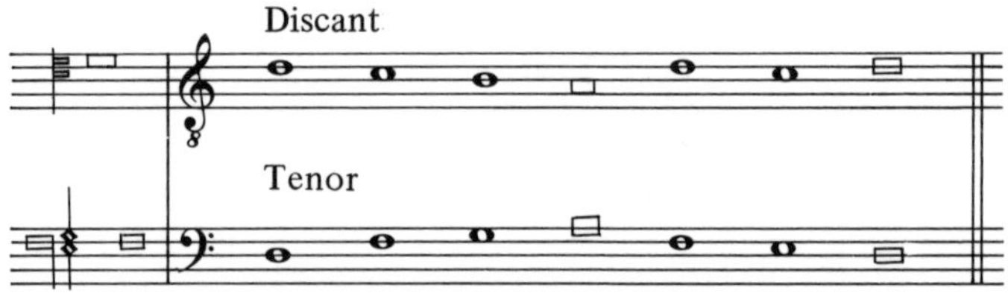

Other cases should be considered in the same way. The reader will pardon me if the examples I had composed for our original copy are not actually shown here, where everything known about counterpoint and mensural song is demonstrated with examples. For they have been omitted through the fault of the printers,[95] who do not have characters necessary to reproduce such instruction.

Second precept

One should take care never to write two successive perfect consonances on different lines and spaces, that is, two fifths or two octaves or two unisons. The same is true of their composite intervals. This rule unquestionably must be observed by every means. For example, if the tenor sings *f, g, a, g* [96] and you want to organize or discant above in this way: *f g,* which makes two parallel octaves, and then another *f g,* the second *f g* is good but the first is completely wrong because of the two octaves.

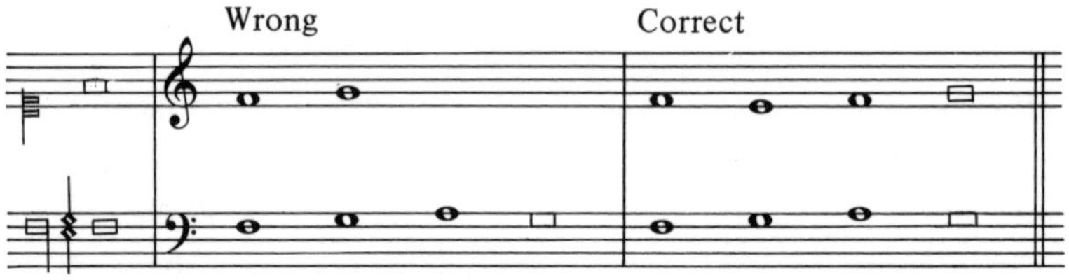

94 The appended note against note musical examples come from the marginal handwritten notes of the printea copy in Parma *Incun. 132.*

95 These are of course the examples supplied by Parma *Incun. 132.*

96 Burtius has *c.*

We can correctly put a fifth after an octave, and the reverse, or a fifteenth after a twelfth, and the reverse. The same is true of other perfect intervals.

Third precept

It should be known in the third case that a counterpoint never ascends or descends in perfect intervals with a plainsong. Yet we can freely ascend or descend in compatible dissonances with a plainsong, sometimes in two or three of them successively, so that a fifth immediately follows many ditones or thirds, and an octave directly follows many sixths. The same is true of other intervals of this type.

Fourth precept

In the fourth case, when you have been on some perfect consonance do not move to compatible dissonances unless you can directly go to perfect consonances, although this is impossible sometimes.

Fifth precept

It should be noted with the clearest perception that you should descend in perfect intervals when a plainsong ascends, or if it descends, you should ascend. For example, if the tenor ascends from low *f* to high *a* and *c*, it is necessary to descend in the counterpoint from the octave *f* to high *e* and *c*.

When the tenor descends on *f e d,* then the organized part will sing *a c d* or *d c d;* if one is not too much a sciolist he will discover the same movement in other cases.

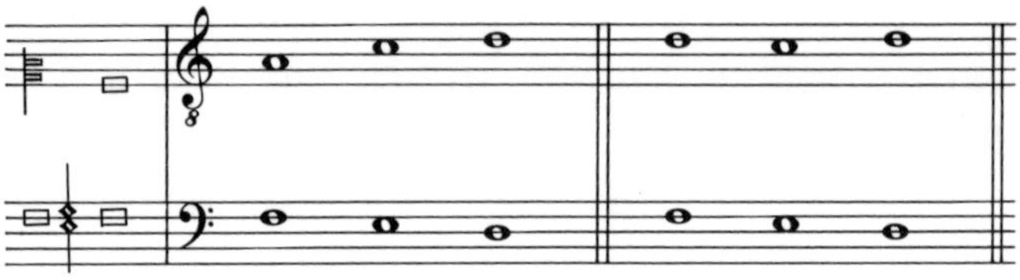

Note that the counterpoint should move to a neighboring interval, as a sixth to an octave or fifth and a third to a unison or fifth. This is also true in other cases. In the best discant or organized part, this part, also commonly called the soprano, imitates the tenor in ascent and descent. It begins one, two, or more notes after the tenor, using the same melody on the same pitches. This is especially followed in mensural music, in which it is called a *fuga* by some practical musicians.

Chapter 4

When an imperfect fifth must be made perfect and when it is naturally imperfect.

As a conclusion to the preceeding let me add this final necessary point. When an imperfect fifth, falling naturally between ♮ *mi* and *f fa,*occurs in counterpoint or mensural song, it must be perfected. For *mi* against *fa* on a fifth or octave never has a concordant sound; this is true not only on a fifth and octave but also on a twelfth and fifteenth. It is necessary to change *mi* into *fa* by using the sign of a moveable semitone or round ♭ . This occurs very frequently with voices against the lowest or bass part of figural song.

It also happens on high ♮ and *f.* For example, if you are on high *f* and you want to compose a fifth below the *f*, it is necessary to sing *fa* and not *mi* on the ♮ by using the sign of soft ♭ .

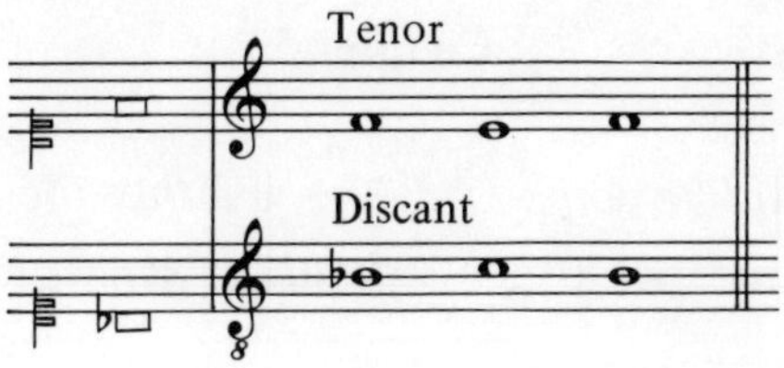

Again, if the tenor is on round ♭ , *on* which *fa* is sung, and you want to compose a fifth under this *fa,* it is necessary to sing *fa* and not *mi.* This is also true in other cases.

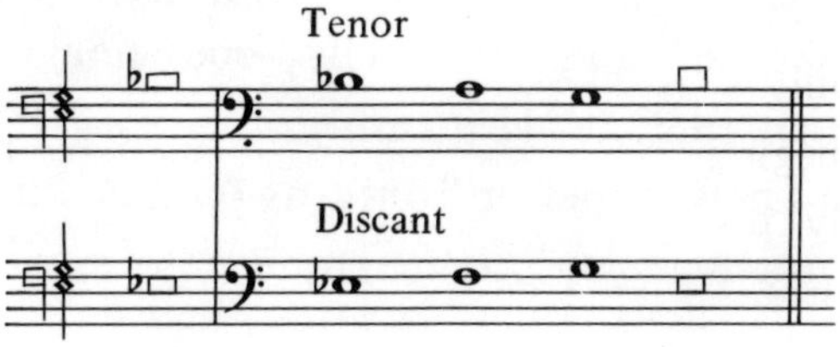

Perhaps someone will ask: when *fa* is not on *e la mi,* how will it be sung? I think it should be answered as above: this procedure was introduced so that an imperfect fifth can be perfected. Among early writers it was called *musica ficta* because according to their common opinion one imagines what does not exist. As they say, we imagine that *fa* is there, although it is not. Others call it *coniuncta,* that is, to make a whole tone from a semitone and a semitone from a whole tone. Some also say that it is the placement of soft ♭ , or square ♮ in an irregular place.

If the sign of soft ♭ is placed on ♮ *mi*[97] or on *e la mi,* it is called irregular because according to Gregorian letters and Guidonian vocables *mi* and not *fa* is naturally there. Thus wherever round ♭ is regularly placed, *fa* must be sung, and where square ♮ is placed, *mi* must be sung. This relationship is very appropriate. By removing unnecessary signs it should be concluded that such signs were invented to perfect an imperfect fifth or octave or similar intervals whenever it was necessary. They are properly called moveable semitones because they are formed according to need, as was shown satisfactorily in the first tract where we spoke about soft and square.

97 Burtius has ♭ *mi.*

Chapter 5

How a song should be composed, and whether the soprano, tenor or contrabass should begin.

It should be known that just as in Guido's hand there are three series of letters, namely low, high, and highest, so counterpoint has three parts, that is, low, high, and highest. In composing a song it is necessary first to have seen many works, that is, to have studied thoroughly an infinite number of songs. Secondly, one should know how to use neumes, the appropriate means of writing songs. Thirdly, it is highly important to know tropes or Tones, as the practitioners say. For from them some produce joy, some produce sorrow, and others cause moderation.

According to the writings of musicians the first mode produces joy, but it is mobile and suitable for all the emotions. The second mode is serious, sad, and suitable for lamentations. Deuterus, the third mode and second authentic, is appropriate in inciting anger. According to Guido, in former times it was depicted in a fiery color. Boethius[98] refers to a certain Tauromenian, greatly excited by this mode, who began to break down a prostitute's door until a citharist changed the mode.

The fourth mode, its plagal, chooses pleasure, that is, it is suitable for causing pleasure and calming anger. Tritus, now our fifth mode and third authentic according to Guido, is called agreeable, modest and cheerful, giving joy to the sad and the uneasy. Its plagal, which is sixth in order, is devout, mournful, and appropriate to those who are easily moved to tears.

Tetrardus, seventh in order and the fourth authentic, is partly playful, pleasant, and energetic; it has varied directions, that is, it is median between each. Its plagal, the eighth mode in order, is more cheerful and conducive to pleasure.

When you have understood these things, compose first the *cantus* or soprano, as they say, with due care, then the tenor, amended and checked for any correction, and finally the contrabass, composed

98 *Op. cit.*, I, 1; p. 184 in Friedlein edition.

without making any dissonance with the order two. Soprano to tenor makes the highest counterpoint, and the contrabass is the low counterpoint in relation to the others because it is the lowest part, as is seen in the following song we composed recently as evidence of our friendship.

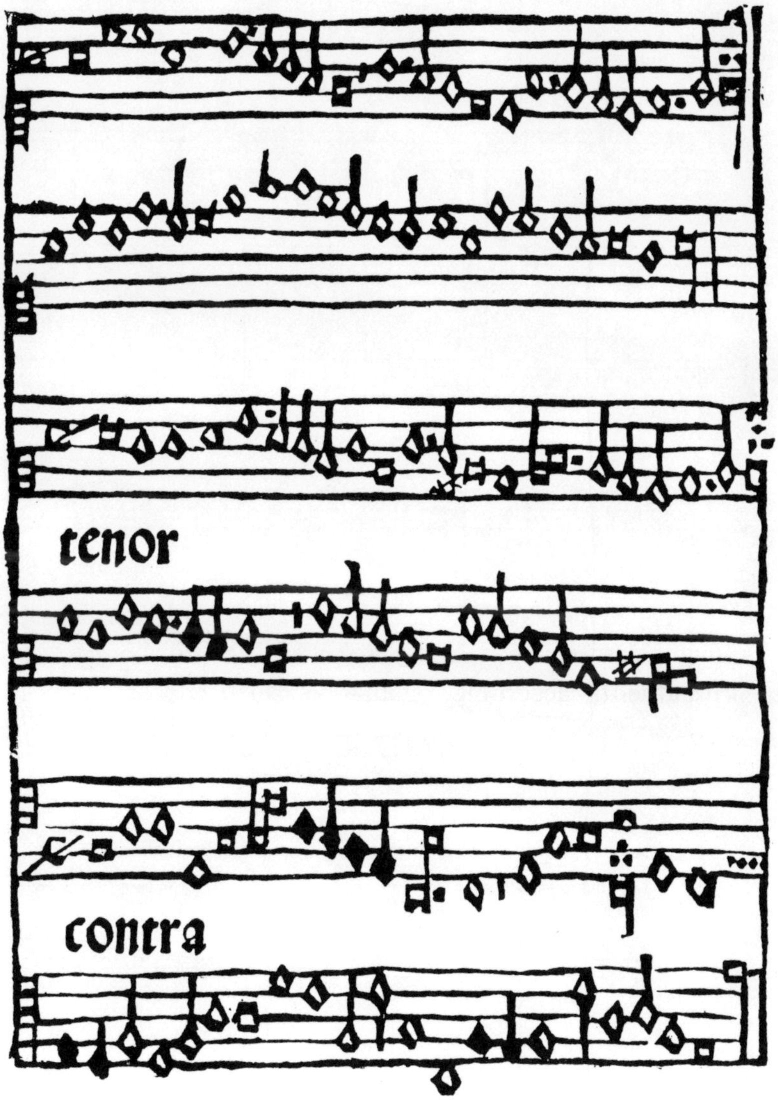

[Transcription]

Having shown the construction of mensural song we must see how it is arranged above plainsong. When one wants to compose a mensural composition on a plainsong the procedure is different than that above, for it is necessary that the plainsong be composed first. The soprano is created or composed second, with great care in regard to the tenor, which is the plainsong. Going from there to the contrabass, the latter must be observed by mind, reason, and eyes in order to remove anything that might disturb the pleasantness of the harmony. Let this be enough for you concerning the composition of new songs.

Chapter 6

The counterpoint of singers and its use among the ultramontane, especially the French.

The counterpoint I learned in childhood, as the Greeks say, I will describe briefly for you. It does not come from musicians, but from practical singers, who in greater measure seek a lower level than a higher. They stoop to apply counterpoint separated from the rules of musicians. It is not necessary to understand here the rules or precepts of composition I discussed earlier but only to bear in mind what is now described for singing.

A unison makes an octave above, a third a tenth, and an octave a fifteenth. Suppose that the tenor begins on low *f e d e d.* which are *fa mi re mi re* in Guidonian vocables, then the organized voice should also begin on *f*; yet it is an octave above, for it only looks like a unison, but in sound is an octave, as I said. Then put a third above *e*; it also looks like a third but it sounds a tenth above. If you want to form a fifth above *d* it will be a fifth to the eyes but a twelfth in sound. If you want to make a sixth above *e* it will be a sixth in numbers but a thirteenth in sound. Also, if you form an octave above *d* it will be an octave to the eyes but in sound will be a disdiapason.

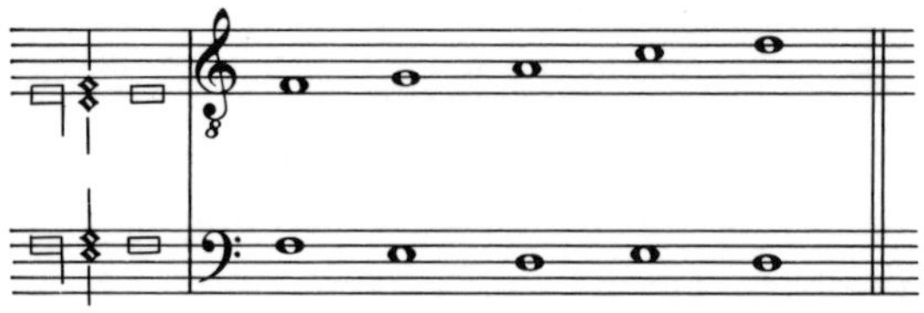

This is the first rule's pattern, as it occupies only the four lines indicated by singers up to the fifteenth, that is, when the tenor descends. You can use this rule in many ways when necessary.

The second rule arises when the tenor ascends. A unison makes an octave, a third under the tenor makes a sixth, a fourth produces a fifth, a sixth under the tenor a third, and an octave under the tenor a unison. Suppose that the tenor is on high *a b c d e,* or *re mi fa sol la* in Guidonian syllables, then the organized part will put the first letter or tone on a unison in regard to sight, but it will be an octave in sound by singing *a g g f e* or *la sol sol fa mi.* For *g* under the tenor's second letter will make a third visually but a sixth in sound. If two is removed from eight by necessity only six remains. The same pattern occurs in the other intervals.

The interval of a fourth which is under *c* makes a fifth in sound by singing *g*. The sixth under *d* by singing *f* or *fa* makes a third in sound, since five from eight necessarily results in three. Finally if you make an octave under high *e*, by singing *e* a unison and not the apparent octave will result. Here is an example:

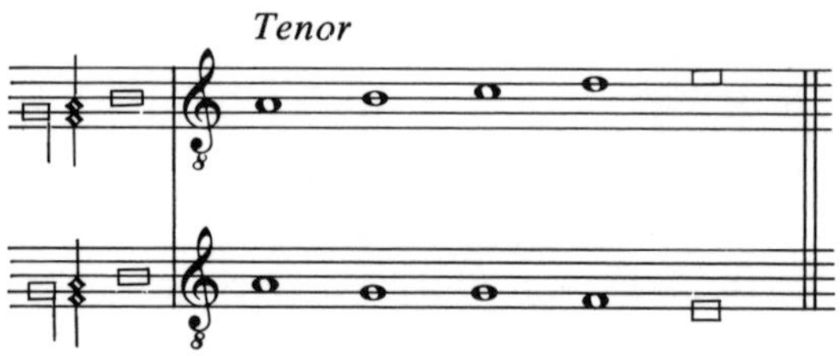

These principles, which are used daily in the chapels of princes, especially by ultramontane singers, I have assembled for the usage of those who wish to organize music on a plainsong within only four lines. They have a very clear application in various ways and patterns. Now I come to the third tract which is distinguished by a more detailed study.

Third Book of Nicolaus Burtius, in which the sources of measured music and the obscurities of proportions are explained.

It is well that the foundations are established, as the distinguished orator said.[99] But we have not only laid open the foundations which are secure and appropriate to finishing the work, but on a very solid and valid basis we have brought the entire edifice almost to completion. It remains only to discuss material that is more highly speculative, following some rules of early writers on figural music, rules which will be explained with due brevity and easy examples. Without such material everything else seems premature, useless, and unworthy.

A quantity, therefore, is discrete or continuous. Following the treatment of figural song our discussion will concern these two. First we will show what a number is and its relation to all numbers. Then proportion, the five genera of unequal proportions, and proportionality will be treated. Finally, I will show with some examples what continuous quantity and its roots are.

Let no one say I question what numbers have to do with songs, because they are known to be so subject to numbers that absolutely no decision about musical movement can be offered unless it is made by proportions assigned to multiplex and superparticular genera. By understanding this you will make music subalternate to arithmetic, since it receives its beginnings from arithmetic. Its subject adds an accidental difference to the subject of arithmetic because it adds sound to numbers. Now let us go to the first chapter.

Chapter 1

What figural song is.

Dearest friends, one should know that figural or mensural song is a certain dispersion of the tones or a lightening of the severity of counterpoint. At first in early time it was not the fashion, as it was only produced in a certain simple disruption of the counterpoint on organs and other instruments as well as the human voice. In that period

99 Cicero, *Oratio pro L. Murena,* 6, 14.

the not yet enlightened talents merit whatever was concealed under the veil of blind ignorance, just as the truth now shines forth and is evident to all. From such procedures, I believe, perfect consonances and compatible and incompatible dissonances became known, also the roots of proportions and whatever pertains to numerical ratios. Afterwards the teaching of Guido spread in Italy and men of truly evident talent saw the simplicity of his teaching as a method of singing. They rejected the characters and ciphers of former ages, which they were not able to do before his time, just as the songs composed and sung at present are not in the shape of Guido's notes.

In current music five principal notes have been invented and given shapes. First is the maxima, named as if the principal note. Second is the long, third the breve, fourth the semibreve, and fifth and last the minim, because formerly it was the smallest of notes. Later more modern composers added the semiminim and the cursea. The semiminim is shaped like a minim, but it is blackened. The cursea has the same body, shape, and blackness as a semiminim, but it is bent backward a little at the tip. A clear example follows:

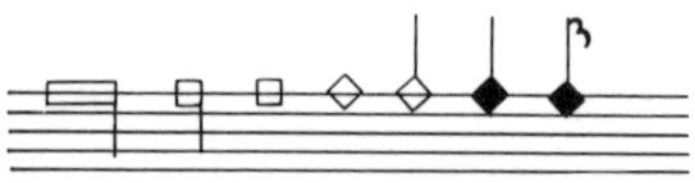

As we said, the maxima has this name because it is the master and principal of all, the long because it is larger than the breve and equal to half of a maxima. The breve is named in relation to the long. The semibreve comes from *semi* or half and breve, because it is half a breve. In the same way a semiminim is named from *semi* and minim. A cursea is named from *cursus* because it moves more quickly. After explaining these notes we have added some things worthy of knowing before proceeding to more details. I will come to the point.

Among many singers three divisions, namely *modus, tempus,* and *prolatio,* are considered in figural song; from them the preceding notes can be counted and sung. According[100] to some, *modus* is named from moving or modulating, but I think it is better named from a measuring

100 The following section is based on Ramis, in Wolf, *op. cit.,* p. 77f.

or reckoning of time. It is also called a union of sound and time measured in longs, that is, the writing of a proportion which arises from longs and is measured in breves or *tempus.* But *tempus* is the continuance of time or the measurement of motion. *Tempus* shows the relationship of breves to semibreves. In a song of *prolatio maior* a semibreve is perfect, but in *prolatio minor* it is imperfect. *Prolatio* is named from *proferre* because time is distinguished better when it is divided into parts. *Prolatio* shows the relation of semibreves to minims. A threefold perfection or imperfection of *modus, tempus,* and *prolatio* is assembled from the preceding.

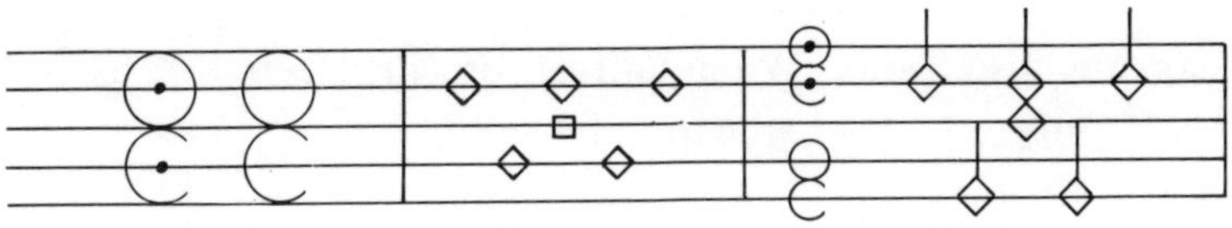

When we join the *modi* together we call it *modus maior,* and on the contrary when *prolatio* is divided it is called *prolatio maior. Modus minor* applies to a long, but *modus maior* applies to a maxima, which some call a double long. *Prolatio minor* applies to a semibreve, but *prolatio maior* to a minim. These things should be memorized.

Chapter 2

How temporal signs are distinguished.

We noted above that *modus, tempus,* and *prolatio* have a twofold division. Now we must see how they can be distinguished and understood. Formerly their division was recognized by different colors, subscriptions or canons, rests, and other signs; now it is through perfection and imperfection. Signs in former times were usually a rectangular shape with three lines for *modus perfectus* and two lines for *modus imperfectus,* as here:

A circle shows *tempus perfectum* and a semicircle *tempus imperfectum.* If both are dotted as, ⊙ Ͼ, *prolatio maior* is indicated; if they are not dotted as, ○ C, then *prolatio minor* is indicated. Also three dots are accustomed to be used for *prolatio maior* and two for *prolatio minor,* as ∵ •• . Likewise, numbers two and three can be written one above the other so that the lower number shows *tempus* and the upper *prolatio.* If both are number $^{3}_{3}$, it shows *tempus perfectum, prolatio maior.* If the lower number is three, and the upper two, as $^{2}_{3}$, *tempus perfectum* and *prolatio minor* are shown. But if the lower is two and the upper three, as $^{3}_{2}$, it indicates *tempus imperfectum* and *prolatio maior.* If both are number two, as $^{2}_{2}$, it means *tempus imperfectum* and *prolatio minor.*

Rests are also signs. When a rest of three *tempora* is indicated, then *modus minor perfectus* is understood.

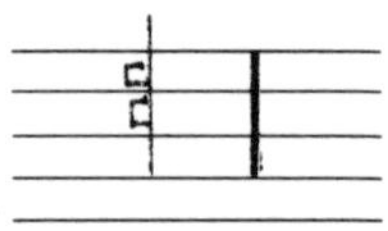

The same is true if a dot is placed after a rest of one *tempus*. If a dot is written after a semibreve rest it shows *tempus perfectum.* A dot after a minim rest indicates *prolatio maior*. According to some, signs are recognized by subscriptions, for whatever is found in a canon subscription must be sung accordingly, even if it is against the art. For they commonly say that canons or subscriptions are used when otherwise a song cannot be sung according to art. Finally a sign can be distinguished by colors when at the beginning or middle of a song black longs are written, also red or white, which belong to earlier times. If they are black they belong to *modus imperfectus;* others are perfect. The same is true of maximas, breves, and other notes. Having removed unnecessary material, let this suffice.

Chapter 3

What a ligature is.

We spoke above about figural song and the seven notes that can be written, namely, the maxima, long, breve, semibreve, also minim, semiminim and cursea. The notes were not connected, but they may be connected in a ligature, which is the union of two or more notes. A ligature is twofold, ascending and descending. An ascending ligature occurs when the second note is higher than the first; a descending ligature is the opposite. I will make some very brief rules about ligatures so that we may move on to more subtle matters. In a descending ligature, if the first note has a stem descending from the left side, and if it is square or oblique in shape, it is said to be with propriety, and it is a breve. But if the first note does not have a stem it is said to be without propriety and is a long.

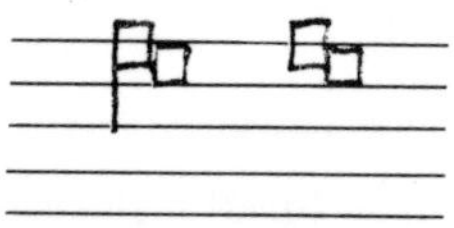

In an ascending ligature, if the first note has a stem descending from the right, it is said to be without propriety and is a long. If it has no stem it is said to be with propriety and is a breve. In every ligature all middle notes are breves unless the first note is written with opposite propriety. Then the first and second notes will be semibreves. The final note of a ligature is written with perfection and is a long when it has a stem descending from the right and is above the penultimate note. A final note of a ligature is without perfection and is a breve when it is a square or oblique shape without a stem and is above the penultimate note. But if the preceding note is written with opposite propriety, both it and the preceding note are semibreves, for they retain a semibreve value.

If the first note of a ligature has an ascending stem on the left side, it is written with opposite propriety and is a semibreve. Propriety in ligatures is considered their property of having a stem extending upward or downward. If a final square-shaped note is below the penultimate note, it is written with perfection. Lastly, notice that every note with opposite propriety is counted as a semibreve.[101] All ligated notes do not need to be counted together, since they can be divided by a dot or otherwise separated. Let this suffice for the present concerning ligatures.

Chapter 4

Perfection and imperfection of notes.

It should be known that a perfect note can be imperfected and an imperfect note can be perfected. A perfect note can be imperfected by removing a third of its value. A note can be perfected by placing a dot after the note, but more on this later. Concerning the imperfection of notes it should generally be known that a note can be imperfected in many ways in relation to its totality or to its parts. It is imperfected according to its totality in two ways, *a parte ante* and *a parte post,* or by a preceding note and by a following note. *A parte ante* occurs when the next note value precedes a note. *A parte post* occurs when it follows a note which is alone or in a perfection. Commit the preceding to memory.

The closest part of a maxima is a long (or its value), of a long a breve, of a breve a semibreve, of a semibreve a minim, and so forth. Thus a single maxima is imperfected by a preceding long or its value. This happens very often in old motets, if you want to investigate it. A perfect note is also imperfected if it alone follows many preceding smaller notes. As already stated, a maxima is imperfected *a parte post* by a following long or its value if it is alone and if followed by many of the next smaller note values. The same is true of perfect longs, breves, and semibreves.

Remember that a perfect note can be imperfected *a parte ante* and *a parte post* by the next note value and by a remote value. The latter also occurs by a remote note and a very remote note. Remote notes are divisions of the closest note value. More remote notes are

[101] Burtius has "breve", which must be an error since it contradicts his previous statement.

divisions of remote note values. Very remote notes are divisions of more remote note values. Thus a minim is closest in relation to a semibreve, remote in relation to a breve, more remote in relation to a long, and very remote in relation to a maxima.

From the preceding I will present some points important to know. In the first place, an imperfectible note preceding itself is always perfect, because notes are similar by shape and not by color. The note to be imperfected must be put before a larger or smaller note, or a larger or smaller rest. Also, like before like, or before the same rest, can never be imperfected, although one can argue against this. A maxima before a maxima can be imperfected by a preceding breve, a semibreve by a minim, a long by a semibreve, and a breve by a minim, so that this is not always true. The answer to this difference is that a note can be imperfected in two ways, according to its total value or to its parts, as stated above. In the first case like before like cannot be imperfected and always will remain perfect. In the second case like before like can be imperfected, for it is not the opposite, since imperfection in this case is the removal of a third part. Thus a maxima is not properly imperfected by an imperfect part.

If two, three, five or eight smaller notes are between larger imperfectible notes, both the latter are perfect unless a smaller note precedes the larger so that it can be imperfected, and unless the second larger note is followed by a smaller note which imperfects it. If between the larger imperfectible notes a dot is placed between the first larger note and the other, or following the others, then the first note can be imperfected. Note that an imperfectible note is one which in itself is perfect, but which can be accidentally imperfected by its preceding or following part, as already stated.

Finally, it should be understood that a note standing alone is counted according to its own value within the context. Also, two smaller rests of the same kind between two larger rests of the same kind should not be separated but should be counted together, although they can be separated by a dot or some other sign. Let this suffice.

Chapter 5

The dot in mensural song.

A dot or point is properly the smallest indivisible quantity of any continuum, that is, of a line or circle.[102] For a dot contains what is best in quantity and most in effect. Among musicians it is a certain sign that is accidentally placed before, after or beween notes, as stated below. In mensural or figural song a note with a dot behind it can never be imperfected.

A dot is twofold, one of perfection and the other of division. A dot of perfection perfects a note normally imperfect by adding one half of its value to it. Contrariwise, a dot of division imperfects a note normally perfect by removing one third of its value. As stated above, it also divides and separates notes from their usual position by making them imperfect through other notes or connecting them to other notes. Thus we can say the division is threefold, of mode, perfection, and prolation.

It is necessary to know that one dot perfects notes and another divides them, so that each of them may be recognized. Sometimes a dot is placed with a minim and after a rest, although then it is measured. If it is put beween two longs encompassed by two maximas it divides *modus maior,* unless perhaps a single breve is found before or after the longs, in which case the breve is counted with the dotted long. Just as this is true of longs beween maximas of *modus maior perfectus,* and breves beween longs of *modus minor perfectus,* semibreves between breves of *tempus perfectum,* so it is true of minims between semibreves of *prolatio maior.* This is enough on dots; let it be memorized.

Chapter 6

What a rest is and how it functions in figural song.

A rest is nothing but the omission of a tone. It is also called a breath measured in *tempora* according to its placement in spaces. So it

102 This sentence is a gloss in *Parma Incun. 132.*

should be known that a rest is equal to as many *tempora* as it occupies in spaces. If it occupies one space it equals one *tempus;* if two, two *tempora;* and if three, three *tempora.*

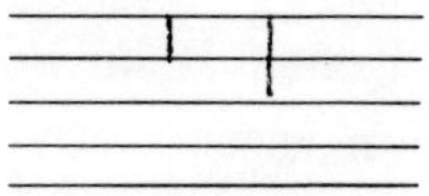

A *modus maior* rest of three *tempora* is only written as a general, unmeasured rest. A semibreve rest must begin at a line and descend to half of a space. Contrariwise, a minim rest ascends to half of a space.

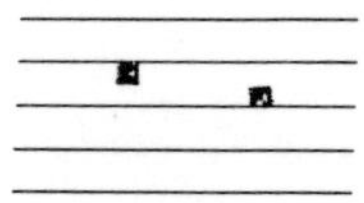

Let me add one point, namely, that a rest can never be imperfected, perfected or altered.

Chapter 7

Alteration in figural song.

Alteration is properly the change of one quality into another. Also, alteration is known according to the amount of its value, that is, it is the doubling of a note. The following points should be mentioned. First, notice that no note is altered before its own size or a smaller value. Also, every alterable note must be altered by preceding a note of the next larger size, as a minim before a semibreve or a semibreve before a breve. Again, note that although a dot put in the middle prevents alteration, a semibreve rest with such a sign has the power to alter. Finally, in older songs be aware that a black note before a red can be altered, and the opposite, yet keeping the other conditions given above.

Chapter 8

Diminution

Diminution is nothing but a certain division of notes which in modern times our present day musicians use a great deal. Some call it singing *per medium* or by half a note's value, while others say *per semis*, which is the same thing. In diminution a long is sung for a maxima, a breve for a long, a semibreve for a breve, and a minim for a semibreve. Rests are considered in the same way.

The above is true if a song is in *modus imperfectus* and either *tempus*, for then diminution is correctly made by halving notes and rests. If a song in *modus perfectus* and *tempus imperfectus* has diminution, then it is sung by halving the notes, so that a breve equal to three semibreves is used for a long equal to three breves. This is enough concerning diminution.

Chapter 9

Syncopation in figural song.

Lastly I will treat syncopation without superfluous detail. Syncopation is the division of the value of any note through separated parts which are counted together. Or it is the counting together of notes separated by intermediary notes. These definitions fit both *tempus perfectum* and *prolatio perfecta* as well as *tempus imperfectum* and *prolatio imperfecta*. When syncopation is in *prolatio maior* it is necessary to have three minims separated with two on one side and one on the other, or to count their value as a perfect semibreve; these notes are counted together through intermediary notes. In *prolatio imperfecta* it is necessary to have two minims or else a semibreve with a dot of perfection to which another minim separated by intermediate notes is counted. The same is true of *modus perfectus* and *tempus perfectum*, also *modus imperfectus* and *tempus imperfectum*.

I would have included many other things of ancient and modern writers, but they seemed confused and valueless to us. Therefore, dear reader, examine favorably what is found in the following example. You will find that not everything is treated perfectly, but retain what is worth knowing. For it would be impossible in such a brief example to include everything from so many discourses.

Principles of figural song.

[Chapter 10]

[*Sesquialter proportion.*]

Following the example of figural song, since sesquialter proportion occurs very often in such a song, I wanted to describe briefly how it can be counted and sung in any prolation. But I will omit a definition of proportion, since it will be treated later when we discuss proportions in greater detail. When sesquialter proportion is in *tempus perfectum* and *prolatio minor,* three minims are counted for two. In *tempus imperfectum* and *prolatio maior,* minims are altered before semibreves, just as in *tempus perfectum* and *prolatio minor* semibreves are altered before breves.

Sesquialter is named from *sexqui,* which is one and a half, as if containing the whole and its second part, namely one half, for one is half of two. Note that when sesquialter is written in black notes without a sign, such notes lose a third of their value. Also, if this proportion occurs in *prolatio minor* and *tempus imperfectum,* the same rule is applied as in *tempus perfectum, prolatio minor*. For in any prolation in which such a proportion occurs, semibreves are always by number three, that is, three and three, while black breves are counted by two, that is, two and two with six as the total.

Finally, note that when black or red notes are found in a prolation, as in olden times, they lose (as I said) a third of their value and no more in both notes and rests. Such black and red notes are altered very often, as semibreves before breves and minims before semibreves, although it may seem incongruous to affirm this, for such notes are accustomed to be altered or perfected, yet this occurs in many places according to custom. Let this suffice concerning sesquialter proportion.

Chapter 11

Numbers and what pertains to them.

Since it is clear that musical proportions arise from numbers, let me show briefly what a number is and some things that pertain to numerical sums. All these are roots of proportions, as I will state later concerning proportions in which consonances consist. According to Isadore,[103] *numerus* is a *multitudo* or great number formed from unities. It is called *numerus* from *nummus,* and takes its meaning from its frequent usage. As proof of this it should be known that a number is threefold:

103 "Etymologiarum" III, 3, 1 in Migne, *Patrologia Latina* LXXXII.

numbering a number, a numbered number, and a number by which we number. Numbering a number is the mind numbering an object. A numbered number is an object numbered. A number by which we number is a discrete quantity called a great number which begins with a unit. A continuous quantity is its parts connected in some common terminal, as a line.

There are four kinds of numbers among arithmeticians. The first begins with one and extends to ten; it is called *monadicus* or monadic from *monas* or one, for as we said, it begins with a unit. The second is called *decadicus* or decadal from *decas* or ten; it extends to one hundred. *Decem* comes from the Greek *desmos,* meaning to connect or join, for intervening smaller numbers are connected and joined together. The third kind is called *centedicus;* it begins at *centum* or one hundred and extends to one thousand. *Centrum* comes from *canthus,* that is, a circle, as some think. The fourth kind is called *miledicus;* it begins with *mille* or one thousand and extends to infinity. *Mille* comes from *multitudo,* a great number; from this arises militia, as if *multitia,* and *milia,* which the Greeks call *miriades* by changing a letter.

Note that a mathematical number is divided into even and odd numbers. An even number can be divided into two equal parts, as two, four, eight, and ten. An odd number cannot be divided into two equal parts, since it lacks or exceeds one number, as three, five, seven, and nine. In even numbers some are perfect, some superfluous, and some diminished. A perfect number is equal to all its aggregate aliquot parts. A part is called aliquot which when taken several times equals its complete total, as is seen in six, which is the first perfect number and the only perfect number in the monadic group. For six times one, three times two, and two times three equal six. But not all are aliquot parts, since four taken several times equals more than seven. Thus the aliquot parts are one, two, three, which make six. Therefore the perfect number six results exactly from addition of its aliquot parts. The perfect number six is within number ten; twenty-eight is perfect within one hundred, and within a thousand, four hundred ninety-six[104] is perfect. Aliquot parts of twenty-eight are fourteen, seven, four, two, and one. From the addition of these aliquot parts the total is reached precisely, just as

[104] Burtius has *quadringentesimus.* See ftn. 42.

with the others. In another way a number is called perfect which arises from all aliquot parts taken together. In this way three is more perfect and exceeds the perfection of six. In a third way a number is called perfect in which there is a rank of numbers, and ten is perfect and the first terminal numeral, as mentioned above.

Superfluous numbers are those whose aggregate aliquot parts exeed the total, as twelve, whose aliquot parts are one, two, three [four], and six, for their sum exceeds twelve, since one, two, three, four, and six made sixteen. Diminished numbers are those whose aggregate aliquot parts do not complete the total but are deficient, as eight and nine. The aliquot parts of eight are one, two, and four, which do not complete the total but only reach seven. The aliquot parts of nine make a total far less than nine. Its ninth part is one, and its third part is three, which make a total of four. Six is not called an aliquot part of nine; since it is not a submultiple it cannot be called aliquot. Another example can be seen in four, whose two aliquot parts are one and two, for twice two is four and four times one is four, but two and one make three. Thus four is a diminished imperfect number. The same is true in similar cases.

Some uneven numbers mentioned above are simple, some composite, and some median. Simple numbers are those which have only number one as an aliquot part, as three has only a third, five a fifth, and seven a seventh, for one is their only aliquot part. Composite numbers are those which are not counted only by one but also by other numbers, as nine, which has one and three by which it is divided, and fifteen, which has one, three, and five. Twenty-one has one, three, and seven.

Median numbers are those which in a certain way seem simple and incomposite, but composite in another way. If nine is compared to twenty-five it is incomposite because it has no common number with twenty-five except number one. But if nine is compared to fifteen it is composite; there is a common number in addition to one, that is, number three. When it is taken three times it equals nine exactly, and when taken five times it equals fifteen.

Note that an even or odd number is divided into linear, superficial, or solid types. A linear number is considered only in regard to the direction of number to number, for a line has only one dimension, length without width. Thus its delineation is in length, as number two, which cannot be shown in another way. Every number is called linear when it is drawn in a direct line. A superficial number arises from one number led into another; it is called superficial because it has two numbers to measure itself, just as a surface *(superficies)* has length and width. To lead a number into itself or another is the same as to multiply one number by another. For a number is said to be led into itself which is multiplied as many times as number one is led into itself. It is led into another number when number one is multiplied by another number. Two is said to be led into three when it is multiplied as many times as number one is in three. Thus by leading two into three, number six arises.

Note that a number can be led into another number in two ways, either once or twice. If once, it will be led either into itself or into another number. If led into itself, it will be a squared number, as twice two, because it will have four equal sides or a square divided by the same units. If it is led into another number it is superficial and not squared, as two led into three makes six, the first number that is superficial and not squared. The root of a square is the number which is led into itself, as twice two equals four. Thus the first square is four and its root is two. The second squared number is nine and its root is three.

If a number is led twice into another number it forms a solid number. For a solid number results from a duple leading of one number into another. It is called solid in the same way as a body has three dimensions, namely, length, width, and depth; so the number has three numbers producing itself. If a number is led twice into itself or once into its square, which is the same thing, it is a cubical number, also called a solid square, and from this it is called cubical. A cube is a body with six surfaces, eight angles, and ten sides. But if another number is led twice into a number, it will make a solid number, as two times three times two forms twelve. Thus every cube is a solid and not the reverse, while every [square] is superficial and not the reverse. It is also clear that the same number is the root of a square and a cube.

A number is divided in several ways, namely into a digit, article and composite number. A digit is any number smaller than ten. An article is a number divisible into ten equal parts so that there is no remainder.[105]

105 20, for example, equals two articles.

A composite or mixed number arises from a digit and an article.

The following pertains to counting, which is the schematic presentation of a number through appropriate figures. There are nine figures representing nine digits, as 9, 8, 7, 6, 5, 4, 3, 2 and 1. The tenth figure is called zero or a figure of nothing, for it means nothing, but gives meaning to other figures. Note that a digit should be written with the single figure appropriate to it. Every number from ten up to one hundred should be written in two figures. If it is an article, it is formed by a zero and a number written to its left, signifying the digit by which the zero is named. If the number is composite a digit is prefixed, which as mentioned, is part of a composite number and which is written on the left side. Every number from one hundred to one thousand should be written with three figures. Also, every number from one thousand to ten thousand, but excluding the latter, is written with only four figures.

Note that any figure placed at the beginning shows its digit. The second place shows ten times the digit, third place one hundred times, fourth place one thousand times, fifth place ten thousand times, and so forth. For a figure in second place indicates only ten times as much as the preceding figure. The first place shows one, the second ten, the third one hundred, the fourth one thousand, the fifth ten thousand, the sixth one hundred thousand, the seventh one million. This should be enough on the different numerical sums.

The relationship of these numbers should not be taken lightly but should be greatly appreciated, since it occurs in many places in sacred scriptures. Not without reason is it said in praise of God: You have arranged all things in numbers, weights, and measures. Remove numbers in all matters and everything is lost. Take away computation and total ignorance will result. We would not be different from other animals which lack reason. We are rightly permitted to have some part in the discipline of numbers when through it we learn about the movement of time, or compute the cycle of months, or recognize the recurrence of years. We are taught by numbers, so let us not be confused by them.

Chapter 12

What proportion is and how many kinds there are.

Above we examined fully the numbers which form proportions; now proportions must be discussed. A proportion is the mutual comparison of two *termini*. I call *termini* numerical sums. Or proportion is the comparison or relation of one quantity to another, which is the same thing. It is twofold, equal and unequal. An equal proportion occurs when an equal number is compared to an equal number, as two to two. An unequal proportion is the comparison of two unequal numbers, as four to three, two to one, and the reverse. This proportion is twofold because it is made according to major or minor inequality. A proportion of major inequality is the comparison of a larger number to a smaller, as two to one and four to three. A proportion of minor inequality is the comparison of a smaller number to a larger, as two to three, three to four, and so forth. In these proportions of major or minor inequality there is a certain difference or excess. If we compare six to four the difference will be two, for six exceeds four by two. The discipline of music includes these unequal proportions, but not equal proportions, for consonances are produced by dissimilar and unequal proportions. Boethius treats this more fully in the second book of his *Musica.*

There is also rational and irrational proportion. Rational proportion is the comparison of measurable quantities. Quantities are called measurable in which a part of the mensuration is exactly divisible into the proportion, as six to four. Two, which is their difference, divides them, for taken twice it makes four, and three times makes six. Quantities are called immeasurable in which there is no common divisor of the proportion, as five to three, for their difference is two, which measures neither. If two is taken twice it exceeds three, if taken three times it exceeds five, and taken twice does not complete five.

An irrational proportion is the comparison of immeasurable quantities. Or an irrational proportion cannot be directly shown by any number, but it can be shown by a proportion which is shown by some number. Enough has now been said about the definition and distinction of proportions. One point worthy of note remains: just as a unit is not a number but the origin of numbers, so an equal proportion contains the first sources of unequal proportions, which we will treat below.

Chapter 13

Five genera of unequal proportions.

There are five genera of major inequality of which three are simple and two are composite. The simple genera are multiplex, superparticular, and superpartient. Composite genera are multiplex superparticular, and multiplex superpartient. These are all the proportions of major inequality; there are the same number of minor inequality to which the preposition *sub* is added. One is submultiplex, the second is subsuperparticular, the third is subsuperpartient, the fourth is multiplex subsuperparticular, and the fifth is subsuperpartient.

Multiplex proportion occurs when the larger number compared to the smaller contains the smaller many times, as two, three or four, so that nothing is lacking and nothing is in excess, as is evident. The roots of multiple proportions are 1, 2, 3, 4, 5, 6, 7, 8, 9, 10. There are an infinite species of multiplex genus. The first proportion is called duple, as two to one, four to two, six to three, eight to four, etc. For two contains one in itself twice, also four and two, six and three, eight and four, so that nothing is lacking, nothing is superabundant.

The second species of multiplex genus is triple proportion, namely, when the larger number compared to the smaller contains the smaller three times, as three to one, six to two, nine to three, and twelve to four. Singers of our time interpret sesquialter incorrectly in figural song by using it for triple proportion. For it is not triple, since three to two forms sesquialter, but they speak rashly about the cipher which indicates three. Since they are very blind they fall into the trap. Now to the subject.

The third species of the multiplex genus is quadruple, namely when the larger number or terminus compared to the smaller contains the smaller four times, as four to one, eight to two, twelve to three, and so forth, for the rest get their names from their numbers. Note that multiplex is named from multiplying numbers of a unit in different ways, as by two, three, four, and so on with the remaining. This genus is the first, oldest, and most excellent of all. For the total results from an indivisible unit which never loses its integrity while proceding in a natural course.

With reason the octave, twelfth, and disdiapason are pleasantly consonant, for they retain the nature of such a multiplex genus. The octave is truly formed in duple proportion, since it arises from eight tones, and eight to four is duple. A fifth in sesquialter proportion joined to a duple proportion makes a triple proportion. A disdiapason in quadruple proportion belongs to the same genus. For a disdiapason is only a double actave.

Chapter 14

Genus superparticular.[106]

This genus is called superparticular because it always has one part above or *desuper.* It is not multiplex, although being generated from it, its parts are complete. Neither is it like a superpartient proportion, but begins with number two, while multiplex begins with one. It differentiates smaller numbers from larger by the short gradation of one part.

Thus a superparticular genus occurs when the larger number compared to the smaller contains the latter once and one smaller aliquot part, as three to two, for three contains two and its median part or one. Four to three contains the smaller number and one, its third part, as is shown in these numbers: 2, 3, 4, 5, 6, 7, 8, 9, 10, for they have many species. The first is called sesquialteral or 3 to 2, the second is sesquitertian or 4 to 3, the third is sesquiquartal or 5 to 4, the fourth is sesquiquintal or 6 to 5, the fifth is sesquisextal or 7 to 6, the sixth is sesquiseptimal or 8 to 7, and the seventh is sesquioctaval or 9 to 8, which is the proportion of a whole tone. When a string is divided into nine equal parts which contain eight parts, the string includes all the smaller parts and especially its eighth part; from this a sesquioctave results, as is clearly seen in the division of a monochord. The relation of other species of this genus follows in the same order.

106 The chapters on the various genera are based on Gallicus in Coussemaker, *op. cit.*, IV, 314–316.

Note that sesquialter is named from *sexqui,* which is one half more, and *altera,* which is a median part, for the median part of the other equal number is added to the complete number, as three to two and six to four, which was mentioned above.

Sesquitertian proportion is named from *sesqui* or one and tertian, for the larger number includes all of the smaller and also the third part of the smaller, as four to three and eight to six. Thus there is no doubt that a fifth is a sesquialter proportion and a fourth is a sesquitertian proportion. Just as a duple proportion arises from a sesquialter proportion and a sesquitertian proportion, so an octave arises from a fifth and a fourth.

Chapter 15

Genus superpartient.

A genus is called superpartient when the larger number contains the smaller once and some part that is not an aliquot part but is composed of two or more aliquot parts of the smaller number, as five to three. For the larger number contains three only once with a remainder of two, which is not called an aliquot part of three but which is composed of two aliquot parts of three, namely of two ones, each of which is called a third part of three. There are many species of this genus. The first proportion is called superbipartient, the second supertripartient, in which a part contains three aliquot parts of the smaller number, as eight to five. The third is superquadripartient, as nine to five. With careful consideration this order continues indefinitely.

In addition to a special name for these proportions, it should be understood how the aliquot parts occur in regard to the smaller numbers, whether they are a third, fourth, or fifth of the smaller number. If a third, the proportion is called superpartient tertian, if a fourth the proportion is called superpartient quartal, and so on indefinitely.

In order to give you a clearer understanding we say the following. When the larger number contains the smaller and its nonaliquot part including the two aliquot parts of the smaller numbers, each of which is a third of the smaller number, then such a proportion is called superbipartient [tertian], as five to three. If the larger number contains the smaller once and the nonaliquot part including three aliquot parts of the smaller number, each of which is a fifth part of the smaller number, such a proportion is called supertripartient quintal, as eight to five. This also occurs proportionally in other numbers, as when we compare ten to six, which is called superquadripartient sextal, and so on in the others.

The roots and first proportions of all superparticular genera are 3, 4, 5, 6, 7, 8, and 9. This genus does not begin with number one or two, but as you see it begins with three. If a larger number is compared to three, a median number intervenes, and thus the first species is five to three. The second results from the next smaller number, or four compared to a larger number with two natural numbers intervening, which are five and six. Thus the larger number will be seven in order to complete the second species, which is called a supertripartient proportion. The third species is formed from the next smaller number or five compared to the larger or nine, with three [107] natural numbers intervening, or six, seven, and eight. Thus nine to five is called superquadripartient. If you continue in the same order with four natural numbers intervening, superquincupartient proportion results, as eleven to six. The same procedure can be continued indefinitely. From their numbers come 5, 7, 9, 11, and 13.

Multiplex proportion of the unequal genus is superior and more excellent than the other simple genera. As stated above, the octave, twelfth, and disdiapason are continued in it. The connection of the fifth and fourth are completed in the superparticular genus. From the third superpartient proportion comes the eleventh, which because of its great discordance is rejected not only by Aristotle [108] and Pythagoras but also by every other group of musicians. Since this third genus does not have the equality of multiples and exceeds the integer relationship of the superparticular genus, it is less appropriate to musical modulation and was entirely removed from it. This is enough on the preceding subject; now we must turn to two composite genera.

107 Burtius has *duorum,* which must be an error.
108 *Problems,* XIX, 41.

Chapter 16

Two other composite genera.

The fourth genus is called multiplex superparticular; it is not useful or necessary for a musician. With good reason its name comes from multiplex and superparticular, for it seems to follow the nature of the first genus in that it duples, triples, or quadruples the smaller number according to the value of the multiple, and because it always has some larger part above it that is also thought to have a superparticular property. Thus multiplex superparticular occurs when the larger number contains the smaller many times and also one aliquot part of the smaller, as five to two. When the larger number contains the smaller twice and also its aliquot part, which is one half of the smaller number, then this is called duple sesquialter proportion, as ten to four. If the larger number contains the smaller twice and more than its third part, it is called duple sesquitertian, as seven to three, just as seen in this natural numerical order: 2, 3, 4, 5, 6, 7, 8, 9, 10. As you see, this genus begins with number two, just as the superparticular, from which it is partly named. If you take three and four from the middle, you have duple sesquialter or the first proportion from five to two. If four, five, and six are the numbers omitted, duple sesquitertian results, as seven to three. If number three is omitted and four, five, six, seven, eight, and nine are intermediary, triple sesquitertian results, as ten to three. This genus can be multiplied indefinitely through further species.

The fifth and last genus is called multiplex superpartient, coming from multiplex and superpartient, for the name is a combination of both. This genus occurs when the larger number contains the smaller many times and also its nonaliquot part which contains some aliquot parts of the smaller number, as eight to three, just as is evident in the normal order of numbers: 3, 4, 5, 6, 7, 8, 9, 10, 11. This genus begins with three, just as superpartient, from which it is partly named. If four, five, six, seven are intermediate, you have duple superbipartient, or eight to three. But if eight, nine, ten and the other four numbers are intermediate, and you compare eleven and three, the proportion will be called triple superpartient, and so on indefinitely.

A recapitulation of the preceding genera can be understood in this brief summary. Every larger number compared to a smaller contains the smaller many times without a remainder, which is multiplex proportion, or it contains the smaller once and something extra, which occurs in two ways. If what the larger number contains in addition to the smaller is the aliquot part of the smaller, it is called a superparticular proportion. If what the larger number contains in addition to the smaller is the nonaliquot part of the smaller containing some aliquot parts of the smaller, it is called a superpartient proportion.

The larger number may also contain the smaller many times and something extra. This happens in two ways. If the remainder is an aliquot part of the smaller number, then multiplex superparticular proportion occurs. If the remainder is a nonaliquot part of the smaller number, yet containing at least two aliquot parts of the smaller, multiplex superpartient proportion occurs. Examples of these have already been shown. Now proportionality must be treated.

Chapter 17

What proportionality is, and how unequal proportions arise from equality.

Since proportions were discussed above, now their divisions, called proportionalities, must be treated. Proportionality is a combination of equal proportions. Note that it is considered in three ways, namely arithmetically, geometrically, and harmonically. When there are only three numbers and the first to the second has the same proportion as the second to the third, and the second or median number is between the three, then it is called proportionality.

Thus there is a threefold division of the median number joining these proportions. There may be an equal difference of the smaller number to the median and the median to the larger, but not an equal proportion, as in 1, 2, 3. Since only one is the difference between one and two, and between two and three, there is no equal proportion, for two to one is a duple proportion, and three to two is sesquialter. Or there may be an equal proportion and not an equal difference, as 1, 2, 4, for two to one forms duple proportion, just as four to two. But between four and two there is a difference of two, and between two and one a difference of one.

In the third genus of proportionality there is neither the same proportion nor the same difference, but just as there is a proportion of the largest number to the smallest, or of one extreme to the other, so there is a difference of the larger numbers to the difference of the smaller numbers as in 3, 4, 6. Six to three makes duple proportion. Between six and four is a difference of two, but between four and three is a difference of one. Two to one is a duple proportion, just as six to three. This is called arithmetic proportionality by Boethius, for the differences are equal. It is geometric when the proportions are equal. The third type we described is harmonic. As in these examples, arithmetic proportionality is 1, 2, 3, geometric 1, 2, 4, and harmonic 3, 4, 6. Among these three divisions proportionality is properly and especially called geometric because the total is contained in equal proportions, but we use the same word for the other proportionalities.

Some are continuous and some are disjunct. Continuous proportionality occurs when a single median number is formed which is compared [to the smaller] and to the larger number, as shown above in definitions and examples. Disjunct proportionality occurs when two median numbers are formed, as in the geometric proportionality 1, 2, 3, 6. For just as two is to one so six is to three, and this is called disjunct. Thus you have continuous proportionality in three numbers and disjunct in four or more.

Chapter 18

Recapitulation of proportions from which consonances and their parts are formed.

When we treated the five genera of inequality, I believe you clearly understood that only three consonances are formed in the multiplex genus, namely the octave, twelfth, and disdiapason. The first is duple proportion, the second is triple, the third or the disdiapason is quadruple, as the numbers 1, 2, 3, 4, show. For two to one produces duple proportion, three to one triple, four to one quadruple. In addition to these three there is another consonance, a fifth in superparticular proportion which is part of the other consonances and which consists of a fourth and a whole tone. The connection of a fifth and a fourth forms an octave, the most perfect of all consonances. Likewise the connection of a whole tone and a fourth forms the consonance of the fifths, which makes a sesquialter proportion when it consists of five notes or sounds. A fourth is in sesquitertian proportion and a whole tone is a sesquioctave, as is seen more fully in the division of a monochord.

I will add some other names of numbers which, although they have the same meaning as those above in forming consonances in the multiplex and superparticular genera, I will list as worth knowing so that you will understand them in Boethius and in Macrobius. The multiplex numbers are duple [*duplaris*],[109] triple, and quadruple; the superparticular are hemiolia or sesquialter, epitrite or sesquitertian, *epogdous* or sesquioctave. A duple number is one which in comparison to a smaller number contains the samller twice, and is called duple proportion, as two to one, four to two, six to three, eight to four, twelve to six, and so forth. A triple number is one which in comparison to a smaller number contains the smaller three times, and is called triple proportion, as three to one, six to two, nine to three, and so forth. A quadruple number is one which in comparison to a smaller number contains it four times, and is called quadruple proportion or twice duple, as four to one, eight to two, and so forth.

A hemiolia number is one which in comparison to a smaller number contains it once and one-half the smaller number, as three to two. It is called hemiolia from *hemi* or half and *olon* or all, as if containing all the smaller and also half of it. This is properly called sesquialter proportion from *sesqui* or half and *alter,* because the median part of the other equal number is added to the complete number. An epitrite number is one which in comparison to the smaller number contains it and its third part, as four to three. Epitrite is named from *epi* or above and *tritos* or third, as if containing all the smaller number and its third part. This proportion is called sesquitertian from *sesqui* or all and tertian, as if containing all the smaller number and its third part. An *epogdous* number is one which in comparison to the smaller number contains it and its eighth part, as nine to eight; it is called a sesquioctave proportion.

109 See Macrobius, *Somnium Scipionis,* I, 6; II, 1.

It is named from *epi* or above and *ogdo* or eight, as if containing the smaller number and its eighth part. Hemiolia, epitrite, and *epogdous* are the names of the larger numbers in the preceding proportions but not properly of their proportions; but since proportions are named from the larger numbers the same names are now given to their proportions that were written for their larger numbers. Thus we call hemiolia a sesquialter proportion, epitrite sesquitertian, and *epogdous* sesquioctave.

Chapter 19

Continuous quantity.

I believe enough was said above about discrete quantity when we spoke about numbers and proportions. Now I will explain some things worth knowing which we have examined very closely in some writers, especially in Euclid. One quantity is discrete and another is continuous. A discrete quantity is not finite but it moves through larger quantities to infinity. The smallest quantity in it is one which is finite, but a plurality may be increased indefinitely, so that a number beginning with a finite one increases and has no end. For this reason, just as numbers are subject to a discrete quantity because of their infinity, so also are sounds, which are created by a relationship of the numbers, as has been already shown. Since they are discrete or mutually different they are infinite, as we said above.

A continuous quantity is totally finite and is also made smaller by an infinite quantity. For a line which is continuous is always cut by an infinite partition when its sum is a foot or some other measure. To clarify this one should know that geometry is commonly described in two ways, theoretically and practically. First the size of the object is investigated by reason and deduction, namely that a triangle has three sides, etc. Then its size is measured by instruments. Its division is threefold, namely altimetric, planimetric, and solimetric. The first is a measurement of height, and is named from altitude and meter; the second considers planes, from which its name is taken; the third studies solids. Instruments employed for such measurements are the quadrant, astrolabe, and so forth. Before proceeding further the theory must be considered, namely, what a dot is from a description of its principal points.

A dot or point is the beginning and end of a magnitude, or the beginning and end of a line. Thus in a line there are two points in its course, namely the beginning and the end, but many lines are possible, for they are formed when a line is divided in the course of its extension. Some have one dimension, as a line, some two, as a surface, and some three, as a body with length, width, and depth.

A figure is a magnitude terminated lineally or superficially. Thus every figure is a plane or a solid. Lines terminate planes and surfaces terminate solid figures. A plane figure is circular or angular. An angular figure is rectilinear and polygonal or consisting of many lines. A circular figure is a plane containing one line called the circumference; from its center is a point from which all lines leading to the circumference are equal. This line is called the center of the circle.

One rectilinear figure is triangular and is properly called a triangle. Another has four angles and is called a quadrangle. Another has five angles and is called pentagonal, and so on indefinitely. Note that in each species there are figures called regular and irregular. Regular figures are uniform in angles and sides, and irregular figures are the opposite. A line is straight whose center does not exceed its extremes; a line is circular whose center is within its extremes. A line which falls perpendicularly is called a plumb line. The construction of a wall is determined by these means.

A rectilinear angle is the distance formed by the meeting of straight lines. There are right, obtuse, and acute angles. A right angle is formed by a straight line falling perpendicularly on another straight line.The perpendicular line and the other line form two angles, so that the perpendicular line is said to be orthogonal, since it divides into right angles. A larger angle is called obtuse and a smaller angle is acute, for the first is wider and the second is more narrow.

A triangle is a plane figure of three lines. Note that one triangle has equilateral sides; it is called *isopleuros*[110] or equilateral. Another kind of triangle has two equal sides and is called *isosceles.* Another has three unequal sides and is called scalene or uneven. According to the parts of a triangle it is divided into orthogonal with one right angle (for *orthos* means right), antigonal with one obtuse angle, and oxigonal with all

110 *hysopleurus* in Burtius.

acute angles. A quadrangle is a plane figure of four lines. One quadrangle is a parallelogram with equidistant sides; another is a disparallelogram without equidistant sides. One kind of parallelogram has all equal sides and is called a square or tessera; another has only equal opposite sides, and is said to be longer in one part because according to one dimension it is longer than according to the other.

A sphere is a solid with one surface. In its middle is a point from which all lines leading to the circumference are equal. Note that there is a difference between a circle and a sphere, for a circle, although round, is a plane figure formed by a single line. Since a circle is completely uniform it is not divided into many species, but is divided into portions of a single quantitative species. Each portion of a circle is a semicircle or a larger or smaller portion in a semicircle. A semicircle is a plane figure conjunct to the diameter and half the circumference of a circle. The diameter is a line dividing a circle into two equal parts, and is is named from *dyo* or two and *metron* or measure. The semidiameter is a straight line from the center of a circle to its circumference. The portion of the circle that is formed opposite the semicircle is a rectilinear figure beyond the center and containing part of the circumference. A straight line is called a segment [*chorda*]; a part of the circumference is called an arc.

When a circle is divided in this way by a segment and its portions, the portion which is central is larger than a semicircle, and the portion which is not is smaller, for the upper portion is smaller and the lower portion is larger. The angle of a semicircle which forms the circumference is called the diameter. The angle of a portion is called a segment which it forms with the circumference. We say that a circle touches a line which extends to the circle at any part but which does not cut the circle. For circles are extensions of themselves and being constantly in contact they are not cut. Concentric circles are those that are written with a common center. Eccentric circles have different centers when a circle is put into a circle.

Although there are many kinds of figures, of all of them the circle is the most perfect, most beautiful, most capacious, and most appropriate to motion, since it is formed from one line. Among rectilinear figures the triangle holds the principal place, especially since two lines cannot enclose or complete a rectilinear figure unless it contains at least three lines, and in such a figure the triangle has first place. A pyramid is a figure whose wide end is called the base and whose narrow end is called a cone. Itwas erected on an exceeding large base which stretched upward to the narrow end. It is named from a figure which imitates a fiery flame, for the Greek *pyr* is the Latin word for fire. Thus, Martial[111] says: Let barbaric Memphis be silent about the marvels of the pyramids. Diodorus also treats them in many places. Let the preceding suffice as a description of figures and magnitudes.

Now let me turn briefly to the measures which relate to this discipline, but also add some terms relative to weights when I believe they are appropriate to the matter and worth knowing. In coming to the subject, a measure is properly taken from a limb of the human body, and everything contained in weight, capacity, length, width, and motion is understood in this context. Although there are various names of measures the following seem especially valuable to know: *digitus, uncia, palma, sexta, pes, cubitum, passus, decempeda, clima, actus, jugerum, stadium, miliare,* and *centuria.* A *digitus* or finger is the smallest of measures; it contains smaller parts, as a half, third, or fourth of a finger. Note that one is quadrate and the other round; when we simply say *digitus* we mean a round finger. It is a sixteenth part of a *pes* or foot, and less than a quadrate by three-fourteenths of a foot. An *uncia* or inch contains a complete finger and its third part, for a *pes* or foot is defined by twelve inches.

A *palma* or hand is twofold, extended and compresses. An extended hand is the amount an open hand covers from thumb to little finger. A compressed hand is the amount four fingers cover, excluding the thumb. When only a hand is named it is considered to be a compressed hand. A *sexta* or sextans contains twelve fingers and fills out the same measurement as an extended hand. A *pes* or foot contains sixteen fingers, and a *cubitus* or cubit equals a foot and one half. A *passus* or pace consists of five feet, although the distance traversed between feet is also called a pace. According to some it was named in this way because feet are indicated by alternate paces.

Decempeda means ten feet and takes its name from *decem* or ten. *Clima* contains sixteen feet and is formed from sixty feet. An *actus,*

[111] *Epigrams,* I, 1.

which was twenty feet, was a piece of cultivated land which cattle ploughed. An *actus* may be minimal, square, or duplicate. A minimal *actus* is four feet wide, which was the space in the fields between neighbors. According to law this is called *servitus* or servitude, for one can not only walk there by himself, but also can lead a horse or team of horses, as at the word *actus* in the book of Pandectus[112] on the servitude of manor peasants, and in the *Institutionum* of the same title. A square *actus* contains one hundred twenty square feet. A duplicate square *actus* is a *jugerum* or juger, which is so named because it is formed from two square *actus* or because it is the area that can be ploughed in a day by a team of oxen. A juger is two hundred forty feet long and one hundred twenty feet wide. A *stadium* or stade is contained in one hundred twenty-five paces. Eight stades equal a *miliarium* or mile-stone, that is, one thousand paces.[113] This is in Pliny Book II of *Historia naturalis.* Finally, a *centuria* consists of one hundred jugers, which accounts for its name. By keeping this name a large number of jugers were encompassed. Formerly among the Romans *centuria* was *caterva,* a troop of one hundred soldiers. Thus, according to Varro,[114] the one who commanded them was a centurion.

The terms for weights are divided in various ways. The smallest of all weights is the *siliqua,* which we call *faba* in Greek. Six *siliquae* make a scruple or obolus, which we call *pensum denarium* or ten pence. A scruple is a twenty-fourth of an *uncia.* A dragma exceeds an obolus and contains three scruples. A *sextula* contains four scruples and is a sixth part of an uncia. In former times the ancients called it a denarius. Then it was the smallest silver coin weighing twenty-four *siliquae,* although a denarius properly contains ten *asses* by weight, and this part, more than the *sextula* and copper *semiuncia,* was the smallest, containing one half an *uncia*. For an *uncia* was named from *unus* or one, because it is one-twelfth of an *as.* An *as* contains twelve *unciae,* as will be seen below. *Sextans* equals two *unciae* or a sixth part of an *as. Quadrans* is a fourth part of an *as,* since four times three make twelve; thus three *unciae* were also called *triuncium. Triens* is a third part of an *as,* for

112 See Justinian's *Digesta,* VIII, 3 in *Corpus Iuris Civilis,* Vol. I, (Berlin, 1954), p; 146.
113 Or a Roman mile.
114 *De lingua Latina* V, 88.

four taken three times equals twelve, and so it is a third part. *Quincuns* equals five *unciae. Semis* is one half an *as*, and comes from *semi,* as it is the median part of an *as. Septunx* equals seven *unciae. Bes* is eight *unciae,* or two parts of an *as*, with the third part taken from *triens. Dodrans* is nine *unciae* with *quadrans* removed; we also call it *novuncium. Dextans* or ten *unciae* is so named because it lacks *sextans* of an *as. Deunx* is eleven *unciae* and lack one *uncia* to make an *as.* So it follows that an *as,* which consists of twelve *unciae,* is properly called *libra* or pound [115] by us. The diminutive of *libra is libella; libra* is also the source of *deliberare.* On the *as* Matthew 10[116] has: Are not two sparrows sold for an *as*? There is no difference between an *as* and a *mna. Mna* in Greek becomes *mina* in Latin by interposing a letter. Concerning this *mna* or gold piece Luke 19 [117] says: Lord, Thy gold piece has earned ten gold pieces. There is also a *hemina,* a measure. Thus Persius [118] has this: the magistrate of Aretium gave too short a measure. *Hemina* is named from *hemis* which is *semis;* according to Aulus Gellius, Book 3, it is half of a *sextarium,* for he says it is based on a *sextarium,* but equals one half of it.

A *dupondius* is more than an *as* and consists of two *libra.* One *pondus* is also called an *assipondium.* Concerning a *dupondium* or two farthings Luke 12 [119] says: Are not five sparrows sold for two farthings? We can say *dupondium* or *dispondium.* After this comes a *sestertius*[120] containing two *libra;* it is also called *semis,* as if *semistertius,* that is, after two the *semis* follows in third place, since it contains two *asses.* According to Varro[121] the ancients named *sestertium* from *tertius semissis.* After *sestertium* there is *tressis,* named from three *asses.* Thus Persius [122] says: the lackey is not worth three coppers. An *octussis, nonussis,* and *decussis* are also found which are respectively eight, nine, and ten *asses. Bicessis* is named from two *decusses,* for it consists of twenty *asses. Centussis* is one hundred *asses* which were small copper

115 This is the Roman of twelve ounces.
116 Matthew 10, 29.
117 Luke 19, 16.
118 *Satires,* I, 130.
119 Luke 12, 6.
120 *Sextertius* in Burtius.
121 *De lingua Latina* V, 173.
122 *Satires* V, 76.

coins. Thus Persius[123] says: he bid a clipped coin for one hundred Greeks.

Beyond a copper *centussis* there is no larger terminology. A lesser coin is the *talentum* or talent, which has various species, weights, and material. It is found in varying weights in different countries, and is larger or smaller. The larger talent equals eighty-three and one third *asses,* although some thought it equaled only eighty *asses.* Pliny[124] writes that in Varro's opinion it was valued at sixteen *sestertii.* If this is believed it equals forty *libras* and is understood from an *atticus,* because it is larger. But a smaller *atticus* contains sixty *asses.* According to some the term talent means not only gold and silver but also copper, iron, and aluminum [*alumen*]. Thus Curtius[125] says: one hundred iron talents, and Herodotus writes:[126] one thousand aluminum talents. This is sufficient information on the preceding material; now let us turn to the measurement of a monochord.

Chapter 20

Measurement of a monochord.

The strings of philosopers have been seen and examined above and continuous and discrete qualities have been discussed. We do not believe that these matters are useless and unrelated to this instruction. For the common and ordinary practice of singers is not considered here but the very careful speculation of musical philosophers. So it has seemed worthy and appropriate to us, now that the bases have been set down, to discuss the measurement of a monochord. Since this has been examined very minutely and in great detail by Boethius, the chief musician, and by Guido of Arezzo and some others, I will simply explain it briefly in an easy way and with modest examples, so that I do not appear as an expert in this matter.

A monochord is given this name because it can be divided with one string, as a *solocordium* or single string. Proslambanomenos is given first

123 *Satires* V, 191.
124 *Historia Naturalis* XXXV, 11.
125 *Historia* IX, 8, 1.
126 *Herodoti historiae* II, 180.

place on this monochord string. It will be a unison from which all other sounds arise, as numbers from one. From this first tone it is necessary to divide the string into nine equal parts. The first part ends on hypate hypaton, which is a whole tone from the first pitch, because a string of nine parts contains in itself a string of eight parts and its eighth part in sesquioctave proportion, from which a whole tone results, as stated above.

For proslambanomenos [*A*] is lower because it has a longer string of nine parts. Who doubts that everything it contains is greater than any part of it? After these two tones are formed it is necessary to create the fourth tone before the third, because a small semitone follows the first whole tone immediately, and because the musical interval is not complete and it does not measure the string in a definite relationship. Therefore, beginning with the first low tone, the entire string is divided into four equal parts. The first division forms a fourth or lichanos hypaton [*d*], which corresponds to the first fourth consonance in sesquitertian proportion. For a string of four parts contains a string of three parts and its third part. Then on the fourth you have just created, we place a compass and divide the whole string into eight equal parts. After fixing the compass on the fourth tone, turn it around toward the lower part and where the ninth part rests the third tone, namely, parhypate hypaton [*c*] is formed, separated from the fourth tone by a whole tone.

On forming the first small semitone

From the distance just created between the second and third tones, a small semitone results that is fixed. For when it is formed according to need or to avoid the harshness of a tritone, as mentioned above, it is called a moveable semitone, but otherwise it is fixed. Every semitone of whatever name must be formed entirely by the compass points of complete musical intervals, since as already stated, it has no equivalent string.

Again, if the compass divides the entire string into three equal parts from the first tone, then the first terminal of this division will be the fifth tone or hypate meson [*e*]. It makes a fifth consonance in sesquialter proportion with the first tone. When the compass is placed on the third tone, dividing the string into four equal parts, the first terminal will be the sixth tone or parhypate meson [*f*]. It makes a fourth note with the third tone and above the fifth interval it forms a small semitone which could not be produced except in this way. If the compass is placed on the fourth tone and the rest of the string is divided into four equal parts, the first terminal will be the seventh tone or lichanos meson [*g*]. It is a fourth in sesquitertian proportion with the fourth tone and a whole tone in sesquioctave proportion to the sixth tone. After this we return to the first pitch of all those formed and divide the string into two equal parts. The terminal of the first division forms an octave of mese [*a*], an equisonant consonant in duple proportion with the first tone.

You, the reader, should keep in mind that a complete string divided in half produced the first octave for you. If you now want to form the second octave and the ninth tone, place the compass on the second tone or hypate hypaton and again divide the entire string into two equal parts. The terminal of the first division is paramese [*b*], the ninth string, which is an octave from the second string and a whole tone from the eighth string. Then fix the compass on the third tone and divide the string into two equal parts. The terminal of the first division forms trite diezeugmenon [*c*], the tenth string, which is a small semitone from the ninth string and an octave from the third string. By dividing the fourth string in half, paranete diezeugmenon [*d*], the eleventh string, is formed, producing an octave from the fourth tone and a whole tone from the tenth tone.

When the compass is placed on the fifth tone and the string is divided in half, nete diezeugmenon [*e*], the twelfth tone, will result. The terminal of the first division will sound an octave with the fifth tone and a whole tone with the eleventh string. If you place the compass on the sixth tone and divide the string in half, the first terminal of the division will give you trite hyperbolaeon [*f*], the thirteenth string, which is a small semitone from the twelfth string and an equisonant octave from the sixth string. Then if the string from the seventh tone is divided into two equal parts, you will form paranete hyperbolaeon [*g*], the fourteenth string, at the first division. It will be a whole tone from the thirteenth string and will sound an octave with the seventh string.

Finally, if you will divide the string into two equal parts from the eighth tone, the first terminal of the division will be nete hyperbolaeon, the fifteenth tone and the last tone of the philosophers, forming an octave with the eighth tone, and a whole tone with the fourteenth. In this way we can divide a string equally in half from one sound to another. From these fifteen strings we can add more tones by using the same process indefinitely of duplicating tones at the octave.

You, the reader, should not wonder that I have arranged these tones in such an order with the fifteen strings of philosophers, since their names are not used through necessity but rather to honor them as the inventors than to use another method of nomenclature. We are at liberty to describe and apply other signs and letters as long as such an arrangement of tones is strictly observed, for when the instrument is plucked we do not hear letters or signs but we listen to the tones of some letter or cipher as mutually related in intervals. Thus such signs and characters will not give us any consonance, but listening to an instrument and producing very clear consonances in division and ratio. Now the division of whole tones by the appropriate semitones must be examined.

Chapter 21

It is necessary to divide all whole tones on a monochord by small and large semitones.

Since we have arranged above in arithmetical proportions the order of whole tones and of natural or fixed semitones and of consonances on a single string, now we must show how any whole tone in this arrangement can be divided into two unequal semitones. When we treated a whole tone in our first tract we showed that it was necessary to divide a whole tone into two unequal parts, a small semitone and a large one or an apotome, which together make a whole tone. Since they are also found on keyed monochords, some called these tones *fictae,* some ♭ *molle*, some *coniunctae,* and some in a better way moveable semitones; all of them must be explained.

Those that sound on stained or black keys of organs and monochords divide individual whole tones into two unequal parts. If you have divided them and you do not find that one is larger or smaller than the other, you will know that the monochord has not been tuned correctly. For a small semitone always results from such a division, not the opposite. Now let me show the order of procedure.

Place the compass on the third tone given above and divide the entire string into eight equal parts. Then you return to this same pitch and place the compass there again, but turned to the left; if you put the key between the first and second tones on the ninth part you will have a whole tone in two parts, of which one will be larger and the other smaller. The larger will clearly sound an apotome and the smaller a small and very pleasant semitone [B♭], an ornament of music. You should know that since this little tone is added or removed at will, for it does not naturally belong to the arrangement of consonances, it has no suitable name. Since it is called a *clavicula* or little key, all with such a name are considered in the same way, and are less necessary in harmonic division except in tempering a tritone.

Wishing to proceed from this and to divide the other tones of the monochord by a small and large semitone as the whole tone above was divided, the compass is put on the moveable semitone between the first two tones or the first whole tone, dividing the entire string into four equal parts. The terminal of the first division between the fourth and fifth tones in sesquioctave proportion is a fourth; this makes a key [*e*♭], which forms the third [*ficta*] tone, just as you wished. Since this tone is divided by a fourth, if you put the compass on the tone [*e*♭] which made this division and you again divide the string in four parts, the first terminal will be a key [*a*♭] which sounds a fourth from the one on which you began, and it will form the fifth [*ficta*] tone or a small and large semitone between the seventh and eighth tones.

If the entire string from this tone [*a*♭], which forms the fifth [*ficta*] tone, is divided into two exactly equal parts and you reverse the compass toward the lower [*third*] part, where the third part ends you place the key [*d*♭], forming the second [*ficta*] tone between the third and fourth tones, for you are dividing by a fifth. From this second [*ficta*] tone divide the entire string into four parts. At the terminal of the first division, between the sixth and seventh tones, place a key [*g*♭] dividing the fourth whole tone by a small and large semitone. This key will be a fourth from the place where the compass began.

Having done this, if you place the compass on the key [*B*♭], which divides the first whole tone, and then you divide the entire string into two equal parts, at the first terminal between the eighth and ninth tones you will have a key [*b*♭] which is an octave away. It also divides the sixth whole tone into a small and large semitone. Finally, if you wish, you can continue in this way and divide any whole tone you find by a small and large semitone through the division of the string into two equal parts, thus making a true octave from one bipartite whole tone to another bipartite whole tone. We leave all these things to be examined by the careful reader, for they are very clear on a monochord.

Chapter 22

Short study of astrology.

Dearest friends, it has not escaped me that I promised some words on astrology at the beginning of this book. For this study should not be passed over in forgetfulness and negligence, especially since I have very carefully investigated this knowledge of stars with my whole heart and talent. For it alone makes us prescient of the future, very similar to the immortal God. By understanding through this study the design of events which are expressed in threatening portents we are able to avoid and escape danger and harm. Since it has been completely removed from the preceding three tracts, I believed that it should be treated here. Now let us begin to discuss this matter.

Although the mathematical art is divided into four parts, namely, arithmetic or numbers, geometry or sizes, music or sounds, and astrology or the study of the heavens and the stars, some writers have stated that this study is not purely mathematical but divided between mathematics and nature, because as they say, it applies mathematical principles to natural things. On this see the very distinguished tract *De sphera*[127] and *De caelo et mundo* of the philosopher.[128] For the world

127 By Johannes de Sacrobosco, written in the first part of the fourteenth century. His treatise had many commentaries, among them one by Prosdocimus de Beldemandis. For the various commentaries see P. Kreisteller, *Iter Italicum,* vols I and II, London, 1965.

128 Aristotle.

which the Greeks call the cosmos we call the visible world, containing sun, moon, stars, and earth. Almighty God created this round and very large universe in order to justly encircle and encompass everything in it. He also gave it two movements: One which is always equal and the same in all respects and which in a way conceals the other that moves forward in some part by its revolution and is propelled in the same way. Besides five other movements He desired that there be an immobile and stationary orb. Of this type there are constellations which do not move in the heavens; they are animated and thus divine, and for this reason they keep their bases perpetually. The names of these twelve constellations are: Aries, Taurus, Gemini, Cancer, Leo, Virgo, Libra, Scorpio, Arcitenes [Sagittarius], Capricorn, Amphora [Aquarius], and Pisces. You will find them fully treated in Iginius.[129]

Among astrologers every sign is divided into 30 degrees. In the entire circle of the zodiac there are 360 degrees,[130] for there are 30 degrees in length and 12 degrees in width. The sun, as if the father of all planets, is placed in the center. From it we see resulting the changes of night and day, the four-part division of the seasons according to the maturity of the produce and the movement of the heavenly bodies. For when the moon follows its wandering course there is no doubt that months are marked. Five other planets follow their own courses in mutually different movements;[131] very few understand their wanderings. Thus Cicero says in *De universitate*[132] that except for a very few, most men do not know the revolutions of other constellations, or their names or numbering. They are unaware that these wandering constellations are the same as what is rightly called time, and that they are provided with an infinite number and admirable variety. Their temporal value can be understood and foreseen absolutely and perfectly from their temporal length. A full and complete year is concluded when the eight planets, following their own courses, have returned to their original position.

129 G. I. Hyginus, early Latin author of *De Astronomia* and *Fabulae*.

130 306 in Burtius.

131 The five planets are Mercury, Venus, Mars, Saturn and Jupiter. See Cicero, *De Re Publica*, I, 14.

132 *Timaeus*, 33.

It is pleasant and worthwhile to understand the natures of planets and the various prognostications of their signs. Saturn, located in the upper part of the heavens, sometimes contributes a confused and burdensome life to man. Thus Persius [133] says: We subdue troublesome Saturn with our good Jupiter. And in Propertius:[134] And the weighty globe of Saturn on every head. In association with man it shows melancholy, its own growth, distillation, and great weight. At times a Saturn of evil suspicion moves men to murmuring. Also it renders a man wholly black or yellow.

Jupiter is the Planet of wisdom, intellect, and fruition; if Mars is included with it the entire science of medicine is represented. If Venus is included it shows the arrangement of sounds, and if Mercury is included it indicates arithmetic, astronomy, philosophy, and geometry. It shows man as white with a ruddy face, fine stature, and well diposed in all customs and manners.

Mars is concerned with heat and dryness. By itself it shows the anguish of the miserable, the shedding of blood, and opression by force. It signifies red men with reddish hair, round faces, and yellow eyes.

In appearance the sun is a good omen and is bad in conjunction under one sign. In human form it indicates men of yellow and swarthy color with some red, also short of stature, curly headed and with fine bodies. By its daily position Venus influences cold and moisture, and the youthful in age; through its powers it encompasses various kinds of entertainment, many unisons, and all kinds of luxury, adornments, and ornaments. It also has power over all sounds. It influences man extending from whiteness to darkness with beauty of complexion and hair, round faces, and pleasant eyes.

If Mercury is not in conjunction with it Mercury is associated with earthly matters and their development, with business men and their businesses, with philosophy and the art of versification. It also indicates man not entirely white but median between the extremes, with a high, long forehead, long face, slanted nose, short beard, eyes almost black, and long fingers.

133 *Satires,* V, 50.
134 I, 4, *Eleg.* 1.

The moon, a feminine fortune, influences coldness and moisture. Through its activity it affects legations, mandates, and the movement of waters. In a figure it indicates a man of whiteness with some redness and with connected eyebrows, also with a round face and fine stature.

Planets also have their own houses named from their signs. Aries and Scorpio are the houses of Mars, Taurus and Gemini of Venus, Gemini and Virgo of Mercury, Cancer of the moon, Leo of the sun, Sagittarius and Pisces of Jupiter, and Capricorn and Aquarius of Saturn. Note that the planets are said to rejoice when they enter these signs, especially Saturn when it enters Aquarius. It is a fine thing to know their elevation, boundaries, triplication, and configuration, also their houses, angles, and especially their powers, in order to be truly proficient in this matter. All this is examined fully in Alcabitius.[135]

The study of this doctrine summons us from this darkness into a higher abode which is clear and very bright with so many luminaries. Is it not good and pleasant to understand the representations of the fixed stars, to observe the planets with their positions, names, and connections, and also to foretell far in advance the eclipse of the sun and moon? This teaching is harmonious and suitable to the human genus; through it we understand the principles and actions of animate and inanimate natural phenomena.

Dearest friends, you have here our little book of musical flowers as I promised. Anything that had been concealed under the veil of ambiguity and held back with a certain ill-will has been revealed and discussed in detail, and as is said, has been corrected with all possible ingenuity. It should be known that what I have collected in love of virtue, which is eternal, with your good will toward me, I have done with very great labor so that it does not leave our hands except as an enchiridion, which is its objective. In it many distinguished subjects, valuable to know, are discussed with clarity, so that through the knowledge of so many lofty matters I think that the readers will be thankful for our constant labor.

Moreover, relying on the judgment of learned men, not on envious men whose minds are perverse, if by chance I have said anything contrary to reason, they will correct it very carefully. I preferred that

135 *Ad scrutanda stellarum magisteria isagogicum.*

some men consider my studies in a bad light rather than to refrain from this excercise and labor. But if the work I have completed is not as correct and clear as I may have hoped, I ask that pardon be extended. Since the teaching and mode of expression is compact, I have done this willingly, and have acted with the need to give the greatest satisfaction to all. For musicians are rare, but there is a multitude of singers who are ignorant and for the greater part unskilled. Thus it was necessary that I use some inelegant phrases and include barbarous terms in the context.

Yet I have devoted myself to brevity and have omitted everything that contributes more to verbosity than to ease of speech. If anyone seeks greater amplitude let him consider himself in the position of an ungrateful man who is not content with things produced with a liberal hand in a modest work. For this book has been brought out in praise of Almighty God, who lives and reigns forever and ever.

Poem to the reader by Nicolaus Burtius of Parma

You who wish to understand the sweet modulation of tones may believe me who teaches with simple brevity, that there is nothing more efficacious for a dedicated man and for the multitude, than a knowledge of sweet sounding song. With it you can always placate the thunder on high, and appease the muse with honorable supplications in your prayers.

Music charms mortal minds and lightens sad hearts with multiple songs. Handsome Apollo was filled with the same music, and gave us joyous songs with his cithara. Also heavenly Jupiter, who presides in the highest stars, and likewise Venus and Mercury. Of the power of melody and the song of the lyre Orpheus is witness, as too is Arion. Philosophers also have celebrated the seven different tones of which the poet Vergil sings.

Just as in ancient times it was honored throughout the circle of the world by many wise men, so Cicero proclaimed the measures of the art. In its encirclement it shines in the heavens and causes everything to revolve in continual movement. Many wise men understand and teach everything through its modulation, and judge verses by a musical measure.

Why do I stop here? In the same way picturesque birds and fish sing joyful songs. Come willingly to the heights, so pleasant is the water of this fountain. And whoever is afraid to strike a serene string, be he young or old, let him assiduously read this little book. But not he who is torn by invidious envy; let him hold his poisonous venom in his heart. This I wish so that our music book may be pleasing to you.

Done at the expense of Benedictus, bookseller of Bologna, and printed there with great skill by Hugo of Rugerius, who is excellent in this art.

In the year of Our Lord 1487, the last day of April.

APPENDIX

Transcribed from MS II 784, ff. 44r–44v,
the Bibliothèque Royale of Brussels.

Note that when the cantus [tenor] is uniform a unison seeks a third and can go to a fifth, a third seeks a fifth, a fifth an octave, an octave a tenth, a tenth a twelfth, and a twelfth a fifteenth.

Contrarwise, when the cantus is uniform a fifteenth seeks a twelfth, a twelfth a tenth, a tenth an octave, an octave a fifth, a fifth a third, and a third a unison:

Fifth to octave *Octave to tenth*

Tenth to twelfth *Twelfth to fifteenth*

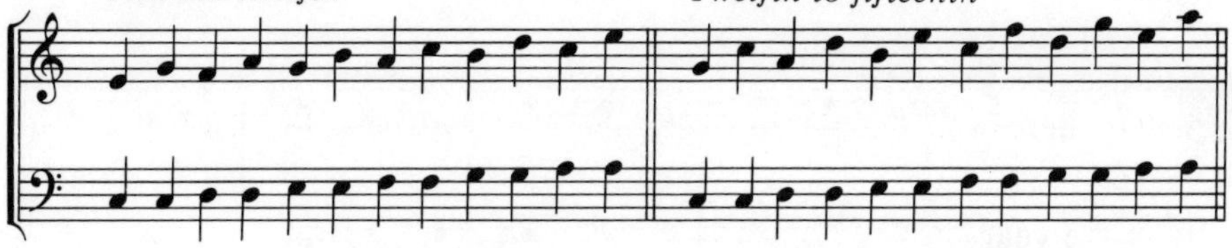

Note that when the cantus is uniform and descends one tone a unison seeks a third, a third a sixth or unison, a fifth a sixth or third, an octave a tenth or sixth, a tenth an octave or thirteenth, and a twelfth a tenth or a thirteenth, as here:

Unison to third to fifth

Third to sixth to octave

Third to unison to fifth

Fifth to sixth to octave

Fifth to third to fifth

Octave to tenth to twelfth

Octave to sixth to octave

Tenth to octave to twelfth

Tenth to thirteenth to fifteenth

Twelfth to tenth to twelfth

Note that when a cantus or tenor ascends a fourth, a fifteenth seeks a tenth or octave and can go to a twelfth. A twelfth seeks an octave, a tenth a fifth, an octave a fifth or third and a fifth a third or unison:

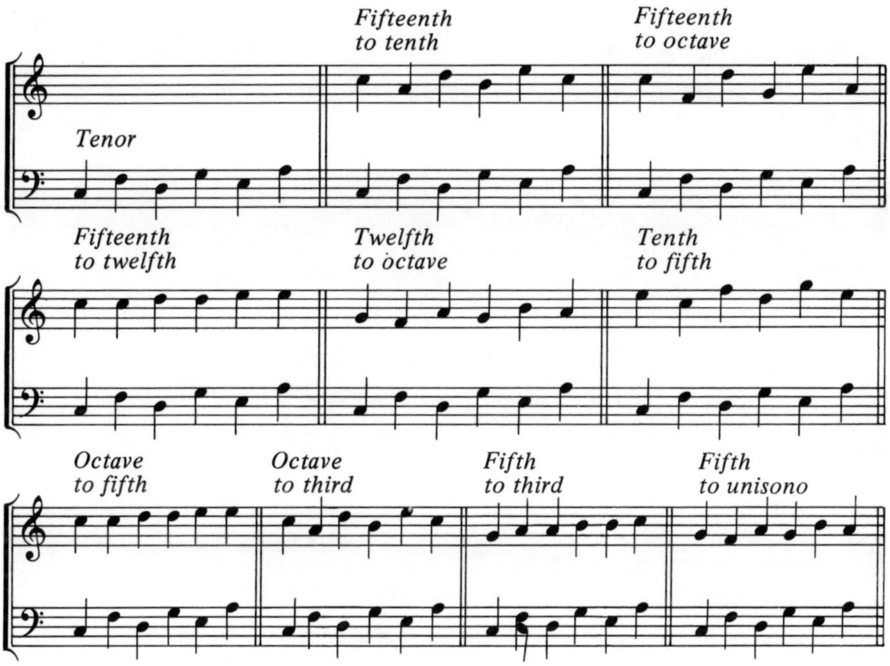

Note that when the cantus descends one tone, a unison seeks a third and can go to a fifth, a third seeks a fifth, a sixth an octave, an octave a tenth, a tenth a twelfth, and a thirteenth a fifteenth:

Note that when the cantus descends a third, a unison seeks a third or fifth, a third a fifth or octave, a fifth an octave, an octave a tenth or twelfth, a tenth a twelfth, and a twelfth a fifteenth:

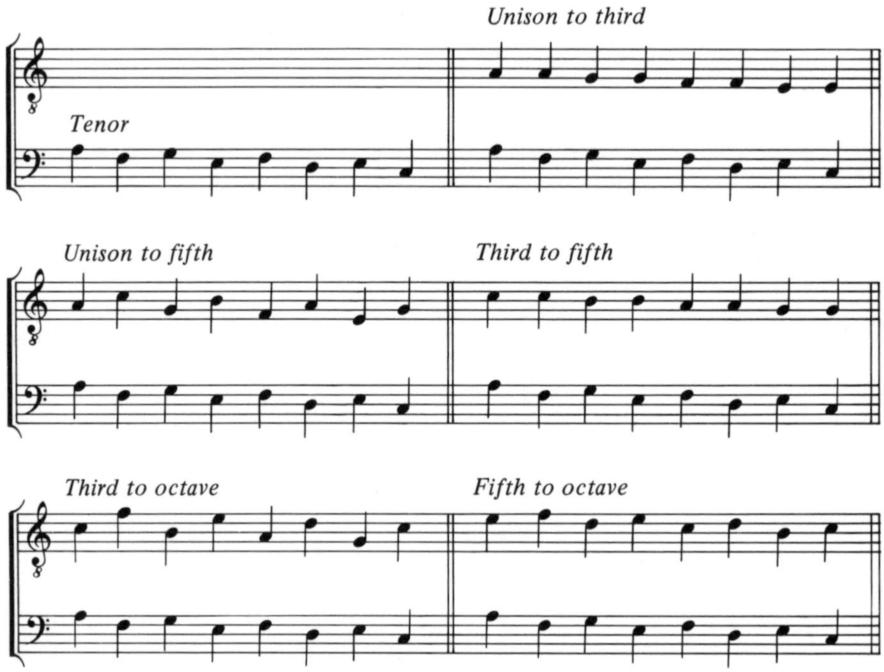

Note that when the cantus descends a fourth, a unison seeks a fifth and can go to an octave, a third seeks a sixth, a fifth an octave, a tenth and octave a twelfth, a tenth a fifteenth, and a twelfth a fifteenth:

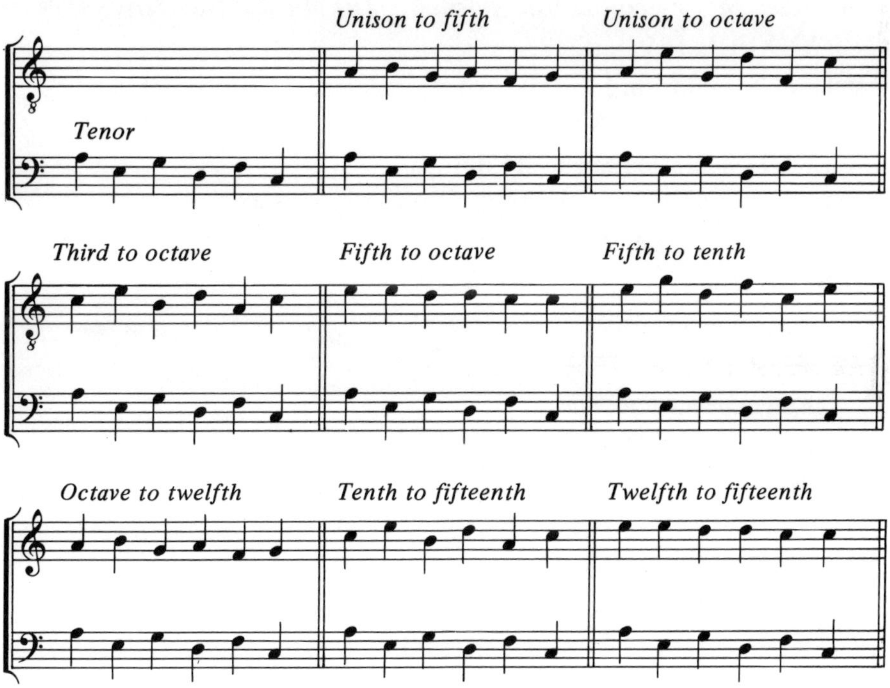

Also note that in ascending, two imperfect species, namely two thirds, two sixths and two tenths can follow each other, but not more than two. In descending, two, three, or more imperfect species can succeed each other, but always followed by perfect species.

BIBLIOGRAPHY

Affo, I. *Memorie degli Scittori e Letterati Parmigiani.* Parma, 1789, 5 vols.

Alberti Magni opera omnia. Aschendorff, 1968.

Alcabitius. *Ad scrutanda stellarum magisteria isagogicum.*

Aristole. *De caelo et mundo.*

Problems.

Aurelianus Reomensis. "Musica disciplina," in Gerbert, *Scriptores,* I, 27. St. Blasien, 1784: reprint 1963.

Boethius. *De institutione musica,* ed. G. Freidlein. Leipzig, 1867.

Bonaventura of Brescia. *Brevis Collectio Artis Musicae.*

Buck, A. "Humanismus," *Die Musik in Geschichte und Gegenwart,* 14 vols.

Bukofzer, M. "Fauxbourdon revisited," *The Musical Quarterly,* XXXVIII (1952), p. 38.

Burtius, N. "Florum Libellus," ed. G. Massera. Florence, 1975.

Musices Opusculum, A 64, Civico

Museo Bibliografico Musicale, Bologna.

Musices Opusculum, ed. G. Vecchi. Bologna, 1969.

Musices Opusculum, Incun. 132, Biblioteca Palatina, Parma.

Catullus, G.V. *Carmen.*

Celsus. *De medicina.*

Cicero, M.T. *De Re Publica.*

Epistulae ad Familiares.

Oratio pro L. Murena.

Timaeus.

Tusculanae Disputationes.

Curtius Rufus. *Historia.*

Decretalium Collectiones, ed. A. Friedberg. Leipzig, 1879.

Gallicus, Joannes. "Ritus canendi," in Coussemaker, *Scriptorum,* IV, 298–421. Paris, 1876: reprint 1963.

Guido d'Arezzo. "De Ignoto Cantu Epistola," in Gerbert, *Scriptores,* III, 37. St. Blasien, 1784; reprint 1963

"De Musica," ibid., II, 43.

Micrologus. ed. J. van Waesberghe, *Corpus Scriptorum De Musica,* 4. American Institute of Musicology, 1955.

Herodotus. *Historia.*

Horace. *Ars poetica.*

Hothby, John. "Three Treatises Against Bartholomeo Ramos," ed. A. Seay, *Corpus Scriptorum De Musica,* 10. American Institute of Musicology, 1964.

Hyginus, G. I. *De astronomia.*

Isidore of Seville. "Etymologiarum," in Migne, *Patrologia Latina* LXXXII.

Jeppesen, K. "Eine musiktheoretische Korrespondenz des früheren Cinquecento," *Acta Musicologica* XIII, 1941. .

Justinian. "Digesta, Institutiones," in *Corpus Iuris Civilis.* Berlin, 1954, 2 vols.

Juvenal. *Satires.*

Lactanius. *Institutiones divinae.*

Lowinsky, Edward E. *Music of the Renaissance as viewed* by *Renaissance Musicians.* Ohio State University Press, 1966.

Macrobius, A.T. Commentary on the *Somnium Scipionis.*

Marchettus of Padua. "Lucidarium," in Gerbert, *Scriptores,* III, 90. St. Blaise,1784: reprint 1963.

Martial. *Epigrams.*

Odo. "Dialogus de musica," in Gerbert, *Scriptores,* I, 252. St. Blaise, 1784: reprint 1963.

Ovid. *Remedia amoris.*

Persius. *Satires.*

Peter of Abano. *Expositio Problematum Aristotelis.*

Pliny. *Historia Naturalis.*

Propertius. *Elegies.*

Ramis de Pareia. *Musica Practica,* ed. J. Wolf, Leipzig, 1901.

Sacrobosco, Johannes de. *De sphaera mundi.*

Seay, A. "The *Dialogus Johannis Ottobi Anglici in arte musica,*" in *Journal of American Musicological Society,* VIII, 1955.

Solinus. *Collectanea.*

Spataro, G. *Honesta defensio in Nicolai Burtii parmensis opusculum.* Bologna, 1491.

Tractatus pulcher. MS II 785, ff. 42v–44v, in the Bibliothèque Royale of Brussels.

Valerius Maximus. *De studio et industria.*

Vanneus, S. *Recanetum de musica aurea.* Rome, 1533.

Varro, M.T. *De lingua Latina libri XXV.*

Vergil. *Georgics.*

Werner, E. "The Psalmodic Formula *Neannoe* and its origin, " *The Musical Quarterly* XXVIII (1942), p. 93.

Wolf, J. *Handbuch der Notationskunde.* Leipzig, 1913–1919. 2. vols.

INDEX